The 99 Beautiful Names of God

for All the People of the Book

The 99 Beautiful Names of God

for All the People of the Book

David Bentley

WIPF & STOCK · Eugene, Oregon

Wipf and Stock Publishers
199 W 8th Ave, Suite 3
Eugene, OR 97401

The 99 Beautiful Names of God for All the People of the Book
By Bentley, David
Copyright©1999 by Bentley, David
ISBN 13: 978-1-5326-5646-0
Publication date 4/6/2020
Previously published by William Carey Library, 1999

*For all of God's Servants who
labor in the Way of Truth*

There is none like Thee, O Lord; Thou art great, and Thy name is great in might. (Jeremiah 10:6)

PREFACE

While editing the final drafts for this book twenty years ago, I was aware that the global missionary community was the intended readership. An Indian edition of the book was distributed along a 99 day walk tracing the journey of the Magi from Baghdad to Bethlehem, Christmas, 2000. Robin Wainwright led this venture less than a year before September 11, 2001, through war scarred Saddam Hussain's Iraq but peaceful Syrian deserts, River Jordan's shallows, and Occupied West Bank Palestine. Near a Jericho Islamic holy site I read selections from the book in the midst of couching camels' gurgling while a group of Arab cameleers stood glancing passively at the foreign Magi imitators commemorating a profound event 2000 years ago.

The 9-11 wake-up calls did uncover latent needs to understand Islam which, in turn, produced a number of books on the 99 Names of God. I can only speculate that this tragedy impacted the message of this specific 1999 book and three later publications I authored regarding Islam which emphasized peaceful interpretations of Jewish, Christian and Muslim scriptures. Both the Muslim and the non-Muslim authors followed the list of the Divine Names which a companion of Muhammad first offered and later credited to al-Ghazali who died at the beginning of the twelfth century. All commentators confirm, as I do, that the Names of God are Beautiful and Transcendent and Innumerable.

During the last few years, I have been working on a publication on the Divine Names that are stamped on ancient as well as modern coins, for example *in God we trust* on US coins and currency. The Biblical and Qur'anic lexicons remain foundational to this untitled book, but St. John of Damascus and other Syrian saints, including the enigmatic Pseudo-Dionysius, are introduced. Dionysius' Greek Divine Names predate the al-Ghazali Arabic list by several centuries.

David Bentley
Long Beach, CA

CONTENTS

Foreword   *xi*

Preface   *xiii*

The 99 Beautiful Names of God   1

Selected Bibliography   101

Subject Index   103

Scripture Index   105

Index of Names — English and Arabic   111

FOREWORD

According to the Qur'an, Jews, Christians, and Muslims worship the same God (29:45 [Flugel ed.]/46 [Egyptian ed.]). Reciting his names has been and can continue to be a means of understanding him and worshipping him more fully. The practice has roots among Syriac Christians who used a string of prayer beads (subha) to help them recite a list of his names. Subsequently it was adopted by Muslims for a longer list, though normally limited to 99 names.

Christians again adopted prayer beads after coming in contact with Muslims during the Crusades, but they were used instead to keep track of the number of "Hail Marys" recited in prayers. This booklet is designed to help worshippers return to the use of God's names in order to understand and worship him more meaningfully.

The Qur'an uses the illustration of a glass lamp in a niche, such as used in Christian worship, to illustrate that God is the light of the heavens and earth (24:35). The New Testament employs a comparable image of the future heavenly city where there will be "no need of a sun or moon to shine upon it, for the glory of God is its light, and its lamp is the Lamb" (Rev. 21:23).

The source of many of the Qur'anic names of God is the Bible, especially the Old Testament. The Qur'an says that God "has revealed the Torah and the Gospel as a guide for people" (3:2/3-4). And God "caused Jesus, son of Mary, to follow…and gave him the Gospel, containing guidance and light, confirming the Torah" (5:48/44; cf. 50/46).

Many of the divine names in the Old Testament are applied to Jesus in the New Testament—for example, the Shepherd (Ps. 23:1-4; John 10:11-16). The names or attributes of God shared by the Bible and the Qur'an are evident in the pages of this book—for example, the Forgiving (1 John 1:9; Qur'an 2:168/173). Others like God's loving includes his loving sinners in the Bible (1 John 4:8-10) but not in the Qur'an (3:50/57).

The phrase God's "most beautiful names" (al-asma al-husna) (Qur'an 17:10), expressing the attributes of God, is engraved on the Eastern Gate of the Dome of the Rock in Jerusalem. Believed by Muslims to be the place where Muhammad was taken on a night journey to the heavens, it is also the place of sacrifice of the former Jewish temple and is beside the traditional place where Jesus was crucified and nearby was buried and rose again.

Centuries later in Constantinople (now Istanbul) there was a mosaic of Jesus inside the Hagia Sophia basilica. As the building changed from being a church to a mosque to a museum and was damaged by earthquakes, repairs were made including a calligrapher writing a Qur'anic verse in the dome where the portrait of Christ had been. Our prayer is that as you read the divine names in the Qur'an you will again see "the glory of God in the face of Jesus Christ" (2 Cor. 4:6).

J. Dudley Woodberry, PhD
Dean Emeritus and Professor of Islamic Studies
Fuller Theological Seminary

PREFACE

On a recent taxi ride in Washington, D.C., my driver was eager to identify the bright blue prayer beads swaying on the rear view mirror. "Allah," he declared with obvious delight, "is great!" I asked this Arab immigrant if he knew some of the names of God that the faithful recite as they finger this *subha*, or rosary as Westerners call the string of 33 beads. He shook his head and clicked his lips indicating, "No."

He proceeded to say that these were his "worry beads" which Middle Eastern men roll with their thumbs on their forefingers, more of a sign of urbane detachment than of any religious attachment.

Despite the driver's reluctance to tell me much about the *subha*, the 33 prayer beads are found from Central Africa to Southeast Asia. Devout Muslims chant the 99 beautiful names of God by running through the beads three times.

A poor North African showed me that he does not depend on the prayer beads, as he pointed to the 14 joints in the fingers and thumb of his right hand. He recited the Arabic, which was heavily influenced by his local Berber dialect, at the same time as his thumb touched lightly the three joints on each finger and the thumb's two joints. The fingering process was repeated seven times and he added an extra to make the 99th name at the close. This practitioner of folk Islam is not alone, as those Muslims looking for a spiritual experience beyond the mosque prayers repeat the names of God in Sufi meetings around the world.

Not to be left out of the discussion of the efficacy of repeating the 99 names, the traditional mosque worshiper is likely to hear several Suras (7, 57 and 59) that proclaim the importance of knowing God's name. These names are often engraved on the walls of modern mosques. There is the hadith, quoting Muhammad, "The Most High God has ninety-nine names and whoever enumerates them will enter into paradise."

Samuel Zwemer reported another tradition which states that the numerals 81 and 18 are written in the palms of the hands.[1] Of course, the imprinted numbers are in present day Arabic script and appear as ΛI on the left and IΛ on

---

[1] Samuel Zwemer, *Studies in Popular Islam* (London: The Sheldon Press, 1939), p.16.

the right hand. Zwemer went on to say that the use of these names and the rosary was a key to understanding Muslim prayers. He felt that faithful investigation of this subject would lead to fruitful results.

My own investigation led me to discover the Semitic pre-Islamic origins for these names of God. Many of the names are right out of the Hebrew or Aramaic portions of our Scriptures. A well-known name that appears in both modern Arabic and Hebrew is derived from a Semitic word that has the three consonants H-F-Tz. The name Al-Hafiz, God the Preserver, produces a slight difference in meaning, however, between the Arabic and Hebrew words. In Hebrew, the HFTz word denotes "pleasure" while the Arabic HFTz word refers to "keep, preserve." It is not too difficult to imagine that God who keeps and preserves his own would also take pleasure in them. In Numbers 14:8, we find, "If the Lord delights/preserves us, he will bring us into the land."

The names of God open up more than devotional and linguistic similarities between Christians and Muslims. The great theological discussions of the Muslims that took place in the early centuries of Islam often touched upon the issue of how Muslims can know God. A great Muslim theologian, Al-Ghazali (died 1111), expressed what has become a fixed theological position. He stated that while it is impossible to know God's essence, it is possible to know the attributes of God as expressed in the 99 names. Al-Ghazali recognized that there were more than 99 names and he attributed Abu Hurraya as the source of these names, which include a few that do not appear in the Qur'an. One Christian scholar, J. Windrow Sweetman, found that the Old Testament and not the Qur'an was the foundation for many of these names.

I should quickly point out that some vital biblical thoughts are missing from these 99 names. As one would expect, any clear reference to Savior or Redeemer is not apparent. The most common word for God's love, *MaHuBBa*, in the Bible (it is likewise found in the Qur'an) is not in these 99 names. Al-Ghazali omits another name that is found in Sura 3, verse 54. In a discourse about the Jews who thought that they crucified Jesus, it names God as "the best of all who deceives." Yet there are at least three names that identify God as the Forgiver, three others that speak of him as the Resurrector, and four that mention God as Creator. God, the Merciful, the Protector, and the Righteous Guide abounds throughout the list.

Many of the great "I Am's" of John's gospel are found in these 99 names. I am the Truth, the Life and Resurrection are clearly defined; but even the less obvious, the Shepherd, the Door, the Way and the Bread, reinforce a Christian interpretation of the rather prosaic English renderings of the Watchful, the Provider, and the Maintainer.

These names/attributes reveal a God who is awesome in the beginning, the end, and throughout all of the creation. He never ceases to be the Majestic, the

Unique, and the Most High. About a dozen of the names are placed in contrast—he is the One Who Lifts Up, the One Who Debases. The One Who Expands is contrasted to the One Who Constricts. Each one of these contrasting names reveals the extent of God's greatness as One who first of all shows mercy, then wrath. As Paul said in Romans 11:22, "Note the kindness and the severity of God." The psalmist proclaims that while God's voice is single, we hear both his power and his mercy. "Once God has spoken; twice have I heard this: that power belongs to God; and that to thee, O Lord, belongs steadfast love" (Ps. 61:11,12).

The unmistakable Unity and Transcendence of God is never so far above all human comprehension that his creation cannot be involved with the Almighty. In what is tantalizingly close to a view of the image of God, men and women are named as God's slaves/servants to most of these attributes/names. The word Abdul prefaces this list for those who want to be called the Servant of the Sublime (Abdul Jalil), Servant of the One who is the Light (Abdan-Nur), or a servant of any of the other names on this list.

One simple solution for the complex question of transliterating Arabic into English words needs a disclaimer for the careful readers of the two languages. The Arabic names are provided that show the ellipses of the "l" in "al" when it connects with a number of consonant sounds, such as "r," "t" and the various "s" sounds; e.g. "Al-Salam" is pronounced "As-Salam" and "Al-Rahman" is pronounced "Ar-Rahman."

The Revised Standard Version of the Bible is cited in hundreds of quotations, but several verses were edited slightly to reflect my interpretation of key words. Three English translations of the Qur'an are identified throughout the text, with an occasional variation in the English words that did conform to the Arabic of the Qur'an.

My special thanks to my wife, Isabel, for her own loving support during the preparation of this book. Also, I want to acknowledge gratitude to Julienne Bowman for her tireless efforts in bringing order to many rough edges of this manuscript. Dr. Frederic Bush provided much insightful help in reviewing the Semitic words which appear throughout this text. Dr. J. Christy Wilson, my neighbor, was also a constant source of encouragement until his death early in 1999.

Each of these showed they were true servants of God and I am indebted greatly to them. Any errors and damaging omissions, even with the help of these competent advisors, I must assume.

David Bentley
Duarte, California
September, 1999

99 Beautiful Names of God

1 The Beneficent, The Sustainer, The Gracious   الرَّحْمٰن AR-RAḤMĀN

The Lord is merciful and gracious, abounding in sustaining care. Psalm 103:8

John Newton's "Amazing Grace" is a glorious affirmation of a benevolent God converging with the human condition that constantly needs wholeness and salvation.

> Amazing grace! how sweet the sound
> That saved a wretch like me.[1]

The name that begins all lists of the 99 names, Ar-Rahman, is always coupled with another form of the same word. "In the name of God Ar-Rahman, Ar-Rahim" introduces all but one of the 114 chapters (suras) of the Qur'an. An identical word is scattered throughout the Hebrew Bible where there are other common biblical words frequently translated as "gracious," "merciful," "covenant love," "kind," etc.

Ar-Rahman, the Merciful One, describes the Divine who constantly reveals a compassionate nature toward his creation. Ar-Rahim is what this divine One does in a cosmos that perpetually requires providential, loving care. The Greek of the New Testament identifies this compassion in the person and the ministry of Jesus, the Messiah. Jesus, the Anointed One, is contrasted to Moses, the prophet who brought the law to the Jews, according to John's gospel.

> The law was given through Moses; grace and truth came through Jesus, the Messiah. (1:17)

This compassion for the world is also found in the words of the Messiah when he speaks to his followers about his mission on behalf of God to be a servant. "I have come not to be served but to serve and to give my life as a ransom for many" (Mark 10:45).

The 99 beautiful names are often used to name a son or a daughter with one of God's names. The name must be prefaced with "Abdul" which signifies servant or slave such as "Abdullah," Servant of Allah. A servant of the Gracious One is called "Abdur-Rahman." One with such a name would be expected to show the character of a Beneficent God much like the parent described in Psalm 103:13:

> As a father has pity (*raham*) upon his children, so the Lord has pity on his children.

Meditation: You are the God of all grace who comes to Your creation as a beneficent and all-embracing Lord. Grant me mercy each moment of my life so that I graciously honor Your name.

Exodus 33:19   Psalm 18:1   Jeremiah 12:15   Jonah 4:2   James 5:11

---

[1] "Amazing Grace" in *The Methodist Hymnal* (New York: The Methodist Publishing House, 1939), no. 209.

2 The Merciful

Gracious is the Lord, and righteous; our God is merciful. Psalm 116:5

The gracious Lord is actively preserving the simple and saving those who are brought low, as Psalm 116:5 eloquently states. There are many names of God that double up to bring an emphasis in meaning, in rhyme, or contrasting ideas. The two opening names are totally wedded together throughout Islam's holy book with the resonating Arabic phrase "*bismallah Ar-Rahman, Ar-Rahim*"—In the name of God the Beneficent, the Merciful.

The two names derived from "mercy" clearly show that our God in heaven is first showing the compassionate side of the divine nature. The psalm writer heard God's merciful voice, yet listens carefully to two divine characteristics:

Once God has spoken; twice have I heard this: That power belongs to God;
And to thee, O Lord, belongs mercy (*hesed*). (Ps. 62:11,12)

God's strength and power are recognized throughout the universe, but that is not all that our Creator intends for us to hear. The voice of the Merciful God does not shout at us out of an earthquake or thunder storm, but it often comes in very humble sounds.

One of the best known stories told by Jesus is "The Good Samaritan" who overcomes deep religious and ethnic biases to offer aid to a Jew who was robbed and left for dead on the road to Jerusalem (Luke 10:29f). Two Jewish religious figures pass the beaten body of their countryman, but the Samaritan not only rescues the man but offers to pay for any additional costs of the healing care. The story ends with this question: "Which of the three proves to be a neighbor to the one who is robbed?" Jesus' response to the one who answers, "The one who showed mercy," is "Go and do likewise" (Luke 10:37).

The servant of God who is sensitive toward the poor, the widows and orphans, rightly deserves the name Abdur-Rahim. Jesus commands his followers to give food to the hungry, clothe the naked, and visit the sick, and warns them of the eternal consequences of neglecting the needy (Matt. 25:40,41).

The Book of the Acts is commonly identified with the history of the early followers of the Messiah, but it also contains many sermons that connect the older parts of the Bible with the first groups of believers in Jesus as the Way. In chapter 13 the apostle Paul reviews the acts of God's mercy in the lives of the prophets: Abraham (v. 26), Moses (38), Samuel (20), David (22,34), as well as Jesus Christ whom God raised up in recent days (26f).

Meditation: Mercy often comes to me when I am weak and vulnerable. Help me, gracious Lord, to accept Your all-sustaining love as a part of Your plan to lift burdens from my life.

Psalm 112:4   Isaiah 53:7   1 Timothy 1:2   2 Timothy 1:2

3   King, Sovereign   ٱلْمَلِك AL-MALIK

The Lord will be king over all the earth; on that day the Lord will be one and his name one. Zechariah 14:9

The king motif runs throughout the Bible as it does throughout most pre-modern literature. A king is a powerful figure in any language, and within religious communities it can only represent the absolute authority that is reserved for God. This name, Al-Malik, appears in the Hebrew Bible with identical sounds and meanings with the Arabic name. It emerges with the first ten of the 99 beautiful names in Sura 59:23,24 in the Qur'an. This is the only place within the Qur'an that this quantity of the divine names are found in one place.

When Jesus warns his followers about not caring for the poor of the earth in this life, he describes the Judge on the last day as a king (Matt. 25:34) and invites those who did feed, clothe, and visit the "least of his brothers" to sit down on the King's right hand of power.

Psalm 110 is filled with kingly allusions, including the requests from the Lord God to another lord to sit at his right hand and to subdue all other kings and rivals (v. 5). Abraham is confronted by several kings in the opening chapters of his life in the land of Canaan. The one king who survives the intrigues and wars of this period does not have much power, but Melchizedek (king of righteousness) is named as the founder of an eternal line in both the Psalms (110:4) and the Book of Hebrews (5:6). Followers of Jesus Christ hold that he fulfills the expectation of the eternal priesthood, as well as the kingly prophecies of these scriptures. Jesus is recognized in a third title, the Prophet, that is explicit in Deuteronomy 18:15.

This King is not an ethereal power limited to the heavens and the after-life but is a definite force in our present world. Jesus introduces this authority as the "kingdom of God/heaven" and spends many hours with his chosen followers explaining this extraordinary concept. Repentance is the first step into entering this kingdom (Matt. 4:17). The kingdom of heaven must be sought before all else, and it is never fully realized in this life, according to Matthew 6:10, where Jesus teaches his followers to pray for the "kingdom to come." This rule of God, the eternal heavenly kingdom, should be sought beyond all other kingdoms and possessions (6:33).

Servants of the King—from lowly, cupbearing slaves to the chief minister—have only delegated power. They are subject to the Sovereign's wise rule and have no other choice but to submit to his rule. A benediction offered by the apostle Paul to his "child in the faith," Timothy, uses the title "King of Kings" with several terms of adornment for the coming return of the Messiah (1Tim. 6:15).

Meditation: O King and Possessor of my earthly and heavenly abodes, I desire to always obey You in all ways, as I have no other Sovereign that owns me so graciously and majestically.

Psalm 2:6, 18:51, 103:19   Isaiah 32:1   John 3:3   James 2:5

99 Beautiful Names of God

4 The Holy   الْقُدُّوس AL-QUDDŪS

My holy name I will make known in the midst of my people. Ezekiel 39:7

Moses removes his shoes when he meets the Lord on holy (Hebrew *qodesh*) ground, a practice that is continued by Muslims when they enter mosques. The Qur'an rarely uses this term. Both Sura 59 and Sura 62:1 associate holy with king, and with spirit. "Jesus, son of Mary, is confirmed with the Holy Spirit" (Sura 2:253).[1] The Bible is a treasury of holy events, items, and persons that emphasize the root meaning of the word as "separateness."

The early kingdom of Israel places great hope in the holy sanctuary built in Jerusalem during the reign of Solomon and rebuilt twice following destructive attacks on the city. Psalm 48 glorifies the city of Jerusalem itself as "the holy mountain, beautiful in elevation and the joy of all the earth" (vv. 1,2).

Following the destruction of this holy place, the people of God come to realize that God does not dwell in houses of stone and mortar. Jeremiah, an eyewitness to the destruction of the holy city in 583 B.C., is given a glimpse of a new house of Israel when the Lord pronounced:

> I will put my law within them, I will write it upon their hearts; I will be their God. (Jer. 31:33)

At the beginning of the Messianic epoch, Jesus introduces the new agent, the Spirit, who will come directly from God for the spiritual revitalization of the people. The union of God and Jesus Christ within the divine mystery will produce a common Spirit, appropriately named the Holy Spirit. Jesus promises his followers on the eve of his crucifixion that this Spirit will be sent by Jesus and also will come from God (John 14:25). The Spirit's coming ensures that Jesus' followers will be witnesses to the truth. The Gospel of John (15:26) indicates how wonderfully and mysteriously bound together is God with Jesus and with the Spirit who represents Jesus while he is away from his followers.

Many of the scriptures following the death and resurrection of Jesus are dedicated to the ethics of living in the Holy Spirit. Paul reminds his readers that while the law is still holy (Rom. 7:12), the new temple is the body of a believer which is to be held in holiness (1 Cor. 3:17). The Holy Spirit becomes a seal and a guarantee of a Christian's ultimate salvation, according to the apostle in Ephesians (1:13,14).

From the beginning of the Bible to the end, holy is identified with detached sacredness. Early portions of scripture emphasize God's separation from his creation, while later portions emphasize human separateness from sin. Hebrews 12:14 speaks for the entire spectrum of scripture, "Strive for peace with all and for holiness, without which no one will see the Lord."

Meditation: Glorious and Gracious God, too often I know You as the Lord of the kingdoms without granting You rule in my life to make me more blameless, more truthful, more holy.

Psalm 51:13, 89:36 Isaiah 6:3, 57:13 Matthew 1:20 Revelation 4:8

---

[1] Refer to page 45, footnote 2, for a Muslim interpretation of "spirit."

5   The Peaceful One    AS-SALĀM

His name shall be called the Prince of Peace. Isaiah 9:6

The current residents of Jerusalem are Arabs and Jews; each group has a different name for the city. For the Christian and Muslim community, Jerusalem is the Holy, *Al-Quds*. Jews refer to the city as *Yerushalaim*, which is equivalent to the biblical name that maintains *shalem* (peace) in the last two syllables. The weary pilgrims returning to the holy city sang Psalm 122. Voices often choked with the stanza that cried out, "Pray for the peace (Hebrew *shalom*) of Jerusalem. May they prosper who love you" (v. 6). The city and the landscape have been changed many times by invading armies—Jerusalem has been attacked nearly forty times in history—yet the desire for peace and a God of peace has never been lacking throughout the same historical periods, including our own decade at the end of the twentieth century.

Muslims in Jerusalem and throughout the world include this term, Salam, in most of their greetings, but it is especially reserved for fellow Muslims. The name Islam comes from the same Semitic root with the basic meaning to be sound, complete, submitted; i.e., a Muslim.

Peace is always elusive. The people of God not only had to "seek peace," they had to "pursue it" (Ps. 34:14); and aside from the promises for those seeking inner peace, this world's promises for peace are more often failures than successes. Peace and wholeness with God came through sacrifices of oxen and other livestock as part of the Israelite's worship (Lev. 3 and 4). The psalmist exclaims, "I will pay my vows, make peace with the Lord in front of the people" (Ps. 116:14).

The great Hebrew prophet Isaiah proclaims the message that a servant of the Lord will be raised up to deliver Israel from her sins and bondage to outside forces. His message is radical because he states that this Servant will suffer on behalf of peace and justice.

> But he (the Servant of the Lord) would be wounded for our transgressions, he was bruised for our iniquities. Upon him was the chastisement that brought us peace. (53:5)

Several New Testament or New Covenant writers follow Jesus' teaching on these words about the travail of the servant. The gospel compiler, Matthew (8:17), the deacon Philip (Acts 8:29), Paul (Phil. 2:7) all testify, along with Jesus, the Anointed One, that the references to the servant were for the Messianic person, Jesus. As servants of Christ and servants to our peers, we have a responsibility to "strive for peace with all" (Heb. 12:14), and bear the fruit of the Holy Spirit which includes "peace," along with love, joy, patience, goodness and faithfulness (Gal. 5:22,23). The two letters to Timothy included peace, along with grace and mercy, in the opening greetings (v. 2). "Grace" represents the highest Greek ideal; "mercy," the highest Hebrew hope; and "peace," the highest universal aspiration.

Meditation: In my pursuit of wholeness and security in this world, may my first prayer always be for peace with You, O my God.

Genesis 26:29   Judges 19:20   Jeremiah 6:14   John 14:27   Acts 10:36

6 The Faithful One   الْمُؤْمِنُ AL-MU'MIN

His mercy never fails....Great is Thy faithfulness. Lamentations of Jeremiah 3:23

Abraham believes (Hebrew *'aman*) the Lord on several occasions. This belief, or trust in a steadfast support, on Abraham's part of the covenant relationship leads the Lord to "count him righteous" (Gen. 15:6). Many years later, at the precise moment of the Exodus from Egypt, the tribes of Israel confess their trust in God and his servant, Moses, for the great deliverance from their oppressors (Ex. 14:31). And at the giving of the law of God to Moses these words ring out:

> Know therefore that the Lord your God is God, the faithful God, who keeps covenant and steadfast love with those who love him and keep his commandments. (Deut. 7:9)

Jeremiah's Lamentations reveal the Sovereign One is a Believer when trust is extended to the believing person (3:23). David, the psalmist and prophet, cries out for salvation: "Do not, O Lord, withhold thy mercy, let thy faithfulness ever preserve me" (Ps. 40:11).

Two of the shorter prophecies of the Hebrew Bible speak of the people's belief and trust. The pagan citizens of Nineveh believe when Jonah preaches to them (3:5) and make a correct response to the call to be faithful in contrast to the Jews who do not believe the message of Habakkuk (1:5). In the Qur'an, Jonah is one of two dozen prophets among the believers in God's messages mentioned by name, which include Moses, Abraham, and David. Sura 10, titled Jonah, refers to the positive responses of the people toward the message, but adds: "no one can believe apart from God's will and he will visit the evil upon those not using their reason" (10:100).

The message of Jesus Christ is directed toward the listeners who will believe in his Word. As with the earlier pronouncements, the believer must be convinced that the Eternal is concerned for his well-being even when there is not much evidence that the trust is based upon a rational choice (Rom. 4:13f). The Bible reveals that a faithful response is not originally based on any body of knowledge, often just on "believe in Me and my Father" (John 14:1,10). Later a body of truth is added that needs a believer's assent (1 Cor. 11:23, Rom. 1:3).

Jesus knows the motives of those who come to him. "Many believed in Jerusalem when they saw the miracles but Jesus did not believe them" (John 2:23,24). Right belief demands an ethical commitment, which is the theme of Jesus' conversation with Nicodemus, a ruler of the Jews. Jesus' answer to this brilliant Pharisee is for him to become born a second time in order to enter the kingdom of God. After further discussion, Jesus challenges him with these words which eventually became the soul of the gospel:

> God loved the world that he gave his unique Son, that whoever believes in him will have eternal life. (John 3:16)

In a parable that Jesus tells, a master commends his servants for wisely using what was entrusted to them. "Well done, good and faithful servant," he pronounces over two, but condemns a third servant for hiding what the master entrusted to him (Matt. 25:21f).

Meditation: My faithful Guardian, help me to be a wise and fearless investor of what You have entrusted to me.

Isaiah 26:2 Psalm 89:2,8 John 10:25 Romans 4:11,17 cf. Deuteronomy 32:4 Hosea 4:20

7 The Protector   AL-MUHAYMIN

The words of the Amen, the faithful witness. Revelation 3:14

This name of God is wrapped in obscurity and is certainly borrowed from a non-Arabic word. The most resourceful lexicons identify the relationship of this attribute/name for God with the previous word, the Faithful One. While the biblical roots are obvious, there are a couple of thoughtful observations which link this word with the Hebrew, Syriac, and Greek of our Scriptures. The first link is the phrase "amen" which is embedded in this Arabic name. A second link is with the character identified as Heman, the musician, of 1 and 2 Chronicles. Psalm 88 includes this name in the title.

"Amen" is the world's most pronounced word. The biblical term that ends all believers' prayers is part of a family of Hebrew, Aramaic and Arabic words. While "amen" is not translated, the other English words can be faith, trust, belief, in both verbal and noun forms. Several of these are highlighted on the previous page. One commentator simply states that Muhaymin means "amen," "I believe" in Arabic.[1] Jesus frequently repeats the word, as in John 3:3: "Amen, amen, I say to you, except a man be born again, he cannot see the kingdom of God." Whenever Muslims pray the prayer of Sura 1, they close with "amen."

The association of this name with the biblical personage of Heman comes from the similar vocalization of the Hebrew and Arabic. In the opening Hebrew verse of Psalm 88, or song, the name of Heman appears along with his title, "the Ezrahite." He is introduced in 1 Chronicles as a Levitical singer (15:16,17) and a founder of a musical order under King David (25:1f).

This psalm is used in the services of the Second Temple in Jerusalem, and in it are several appeals to the Lord for help, including the first verse in the English translations: "O Lord, my God, I call for help by day; I cry out in the night before thee" (88:1). From the Pit, the depths of despair, the call continued:

> Is thy steadfast love (Hebrew, *hesed*) declared in the grave? Or thy faithfulness (*'amoun*) in Abbadon? Are thy wonders known in the darkness, Or thy saving help in the land of forgetfulness? (11,12)

We can only speculate whether Heman was a choir director or poet who wrote the lyrics for this Hebrew hymn. He would know, as most of his fellow Jews would know, the despair of his people when they faced constant national as well as personal threats. As a servant of God, he trusted in his Protector to get him through the difficult times.

Meditation: I believe. Amen. You, O Creator, are my true Guardian.

---

1 Chronicles 16:36 2 Chronicles 5:12, 20:20 Revelation 22:20

---

[1] Hans Wehr, *A Dictionary of Modern Arabic* (Weisbaden: Harrassowitz, 1961), p. 1044.

8   The Strong One  AL-'AZIZ

Turn and take pity on me; give thy strength to thy servant. Psalm 86:16

Al-Aziz and the following name are among several in this list that mention God as the possessor of might, power and strength. All of these names have Hebrew equivalent vocalizations. A rich collection of words in both Semitic languages indicate might and strength. *Gadol* is a favorite word in the Hebrew Bible but does not have an Arabic equivalent. "O great and mighty God whose name is the Lord of hosts, great in counsel and mighty in deed" (Jer. 32:18).

The Book of Psalms, with all its human pathos, directs the reader/listener to the powerful God who is able to overcome the attacks of one's enemies. David, the prophet and compiler-author of many of these psalms, entreats the God of Victory to show mercy on him. In Psalm 86, David addresses God as One who is good and forgiving (v. 5) and calls himself God's servant:

> Turn to me and show mercy on me; Give thy strength (Hebrew, '*azz*) to thy servant. (16)

The theme of the Mighty God responding to the cries of the people is found in another text of David:

> O Lord, my Lord, my Strength, you have covered my head in the day of battle. (140:7)

Finally from this same author, the word of assurance generates strength in the supplicant's cry:

> On the day I called, you answered me, My strength of soul you did increase. (138:3)

The word '*aziz* stems from a military term designating a fort or armed city. The spies who are sent to Canaan and report back to Moses and Aaron give a majority view that the people are fierce and the cities fortified (Num. 13:28). Yet once Moses faces the sea at the Exodus crossing, a strong east wind works in his favor to make the sea become dry land and enables the Israelites to cross over to safety (Ex. 14:21). Moses joins the tribes of Israel in song after this mighty deed, "The Lord is my strength and he has become my salvation" (Ex. 15:2).

Another song is recorded by Isaiah that will be sung in the land of Judah at a future date:

> We have a strong city; He sets up salvation as walls and bulwarks. (Isa. 26:1)

The Magnificat of Mary, mother to Jesus, provides a song of praise to the Mighty God, "He has shown his strength with his arm" (Luke 1:51). The Greek word for strength also has a military source (*krateo*) but Paul used it as meaning "mightily strengthened through the Holy Spirit" (Eph. 3:16).

Meditation: Surround Your servants with Your mighty arm, O Sovereign Lord. Deliver them from their enemies within their souls according to Your merciful name.

Isaiah 40:26,29   Psalm 8:3   2 Timothy 4:17   Revelation 3:2

9   The Mighty One, Compeller   ٱلْجَبَّارُ   AL-JABBĀR

And his name will be called...Mighty God. Isaiah 9:6

Absolute strength and might in the hands of the beneficent Creator is one thing; but give the same power to mortals and the equation quickly changes. Jabbar (Hebrew *gabbor*) defines God and courageous men of strength. Cush "was the first on earth to be a mighty man" and his son, Nimrod, "was a mighty hunter before the Lord" (Gen. 10:8,9). Scores of "mighty men" are named throughout the Hebrew records, which included the Syrian Naaman (2 Kings 5:1). Naaman's wife is a *gaborah* to the captive slave girl (5:3). Likewise, Sarah is referred to as a mistress by her handmaiden, Hagar (Gen. 16:8), with a similar mistress-slave relationship mentioned in Psalm 123:2. The Canaanite fortified city, Gibeon, prior to Joshua's cunning attack, is described as a great city (Josh. 10:2).

In times of stress even the mighty men will crumble. A few of these human champions turn to work evil. Goliath is slain by David, which leads to further defeats for David's traditional enemies (1 Sam. 17:51). Isaiah mocks the haughty champions who no longer can tell the difference between good and evil and are "mighty at drinking wine" (Isa. 5:22).

The future for the people of Israel will be their return to the mighty God (Isa. 10:21) who was exalted in Psalm 24:

> Who is the King of glory? The Lord, strong and mighty, The Lord, mighty in battle. (v. 8)

Many of the same questions regarding this Messiah-King are answered at the triumphal entry of Jesus, the Messiah, when he enters Jerusalem to begin his passion week (Luke 19:28f).

Several accounts in the Gospels and Epistles tell of the mighty works that Jesus did while he lived on earth (Matt. 11:20f) which were also performed by the strength of the Holy Spirit in apostolic times, according to Romans 15:18,19.

Many Muslims quote the verse in the Qur'an that states there is "no compulsion in matters of religion" (Sura 2:256). There are problems with the interpretation of this verse out of the Qur'anic context. One of the more serious issues involves a deterministic deity who acts compulsively to overcome human frailties. Another question about this verse is whether this non-compulsory text has been abrogated by later Qur'anic teachings, indicating that force is acceptable in religion (cf. names 69 and 70).

Meditation: You O mighty King, and I the servant are joined together to fulfill Your gracious will. But in Your infinitely wise creation You have endowed Your servant with freedom. Help me to match my freedom with Your will in Your kingdom.

Deuteronomy 10:17   Jeremiah 46:6   Joel 2:7   Luke 1:49   Ephesians 1:19

10 Most Great, Proud   المُتَكَبِّر AL-MUTAKABBIR

There is none like God, who rides through the heavens to help and in his Greatness through the skies. Deuteronomy 33:26

Pride and haughty spirits are condemned throughout the pages of the Bible. "Haughty eyes" are the first of the seven deadly sins listed in Proverbs 6:17. Pride is condemned in the Gospel of Mark along with evil eye, blasphemy, foolishness, etc. (7:22). The titles listed for this name of God include the expression "God is One who has a right to be proud." This attribute is the emphatic form of another name, Al-Kabir (number 37), which means Great. The cries of Muslims shouting, "Allah akbar," "God is greater..." send a mixed message of devotion, faith, and fear to those in earshot of these militant voices.

Like all of these names, the Proud One is communicable to his creation but at great risks because humans can absorb only one of these attributes at a time. God blends each of these names together so that he represents perfection; but his creation is not capable of balancing these attributes, and someone who may worthily be called proud moves quickly to arrogance.

God's name is called out in the public squares of many nations of the world. God is Great! God is Greater than... (part of the phrase can be filled in or left unsaid). God is Most Great!

A most great God is not proud. He is majestic! The specific Hebrew word (*ga'oun*) is not related to the Arabic word in terms of word origins, yet both revel in the fact that God is worthy of praise and majesty. Pride and haughtiness describe only humanity.

The Bible describes a number of nations arrogant because of their wealth and power: Egyptians (Ezek. 32:12), Chaldeans (Isa. 13:11) and Philistines (Zech. 9:6). All are condemned for their pride.

Elsewhere the word has the simple meaning of "many" (waters in Isa. 17:13),"much" (wind in Job 1:19), "quantities" (food in Job 36:31) and "distance" (Gen. 37:18).

The Epistle of Peter is addressed to a pastoral group in the Anatolian region of present-day Turkey. Peter concludes his comments to the servants with warnings against pride:
> God opposes the proud but gives grace to the humble. Humble yourselves therefore under the mighty hand of God, that in due time he may exalt you. (1 Peter 5:5,6)

Meditation: Majesty and Greatness belong to You, O God. My proud thoughts soar up to Your heights and my appetites are unsettled. Only You, O Exalted One, can save me from pride.

Job 31:25, 34:37, 35:16 Psalm 76:12, 103:11 Luke 1:51 Romans 1:30

11 Creator   اَلْخَالِقُ AL-KHĀLIQ

In the beginning God created the heavens and the earth. Genesis 1:1

This name is the first of three in succession and a later name that praise God as the Creator of the universe. The name Al-Khaliq is mentioned throughout the Arabic Bible while the Hebrew *Al-Bari* identification prevails in that language, as in Genesis 1:1.

Creation in the Qur'an flows out of the biblical tradition of taking place in six days, although there is no uniform interpretation of what kind of time these six days represent (Suras 7:54 and 57:4).

God's great work in creation is passed along to creatures who are able to reproduce "after their kind" (Gen. 1:22,25) and to Adam, created in the image of God from earthly materials. God not only tells him to be fruitful, but gives him dominion over all living things (1:28). God bestows his creative powers upon Adam, with the difference that Adam is unable to create from nothing.

The Qur'an expands upon Adam's naming of the other creatures God has formed (Gen. 2:20). When Adam succeeds in naming all of the creatures and thus reveals God's hidden mysteries, God commands all the angels to bow down to Adam. All prostrate themselves except for Iblis, a name for Satan, who refuses because he is proud (Sura 2:33).

Much has been written about Adam's knowledge of the names of all things, including the names of God, which reveals not only the beginning of rational thought but the beginning of proper worship. The Creator, not the creature, is the proper object of worship. Paul reminds his Roman readers about the effects of improper worship:

> God gave them up in the lusts of their hearts...because they exchanged the truth about God and worshipped and served the creature rather than the Creator, who is blessed for ever! Amen. (Rom. 1:24,25)

Creature and idol worship was rife during Bible times despite the first and second commandments' admonishments against them: "You shall have no other gods before me" (Deut. 5:7). Isaiah contrasts the pristine act of creation with the decadent idol worship of his day that will finally destroy the Jewish nation. The prophet offers the mercy of God:

> The Lord says, he who created you, and formed you, O Israel: Fear not, for I have redeemed you. (Isa. 43:1,2)

The vision of Isaiah does not end with the destruction of his beloved Judah and Jerusalem. He is given a glimpse of the Messianic age: "Lo, I create new heavens and a new earth" (65:17). The new age is launched by the coming of Jesus, introduced by John in his Gospel as the Word: "In the beginning was the Word and the Word was with God" (1:1).

The servant of the Creator God cannot create from nothing as God did. Any attempt to do this is an act of idolatry. The servant knows that his or her position is derived from these promises:

> If anyone is in Christ, he is a new creation, the old has passed away. Lo, the new has come. (2 Cor. 5:17)

Meditation: You have created me and all of the human race out of love and compassion. Help me, O Creator, to reflect Your image.

Genesis 5:1 Psalm 51:10 Jeremiah 31:22 Ephesians 2:10 1 Peter 5:19

99 Beautiful Names of God

12 The Maker, The Creator ٱلْبَارِئُ AL-BĀRI'

Have we not all one Father? Has not one God created us? Malachi 2:10

Creator and creation references reveal that the names Al-Khaliq and Al-Bari (11 and 12) are interchangeable in the biblical texts.

Humanity is the crown of Creation and Adam's ability to name all creatures has been hailed as the apex of both God's creation and the intellectual skills of humankind. Our first parents would go on to freely worship God as the Creator, but the temptation by the Evil One, Satan, leads them to use their divinely given freedom to reject God's word. Jews, Christians and Muslims are fairly much in agreement with these broad sketches of the creation of Adam from Genesis 3 and Suras 2:31f, 20:115f and 7:24f.

Muslims insist that the temptation is limited to our first father and mother and that there is no inherited transgression that is passed along to all future generations, commonly known as original sin. The biblical records indicate that sin will become a menacing factor for all—great as well as lesser-known characters will fall into sin. The prophets after Adam, Noah, Abraham, Moses and David, are no exceptions; all are recognized in the Bible as sinful and needing the Creator's forgiveness.

Prior to the flood at the time of Noah, the Lord sees the progress of evil and announces, "I will destroy man whom I have created" (Gen. 6:7). Moses recalls the great mercy of God in the day of creation, and the redemption of the children of Israel from Egypt, to warn them against the sin of idolatry (Deut. 4:32f). Yet the nation of Israel becomes a prototype of collective sin and guilt.

God's holy character, separated from the created cosmos, would be satisfied by a system of covenants and sacrifices. The conditions for these animal sacrifices which are described in the Book of Leviticus become part of the temple worship in Jerusalem (Lev. 7:1-10). Yet it is this sacrificial system that God and his prophets will condemn as the most thoroughly corrupted form of worship. Isaiah cries out against idolatry:

> Woe to him who strives with his Maker, an earthen vessel with the potter!
> Does the clay say to him who fashions it, "What are you making?" (Isa. 45:9)

Jeremiah's view of the burning of the temple recalls "the sins of the prophets, the iniquities of the priests" (Lam. 4:13). Hosea, the prophet of eighth-century Israel, sees the day coming when the sacrifices will end (3:4).

The apostle Paul's letter to the Ephesians places the action of the God of Creation in Jesus Christ who "reveals God's mystery hidden for ages" (3:9). A servant of God is "created in Christ Jesus for good works" (2:10) and the servant assumes a "new nature, created after the likeness of God in true righteousness and holiness" (4:24).

Meditation: O wonderful Maker of the heavens and the earth, answer my prayer as You did for David and create in me a clean heart.

Psalm 51:10 Isaiah 41:20, 45:7 Jeremiah 31:22 1 Peter 4:19 Colossians 1:16

13 The Fashioner   ٱلْمُصَوِّر AL-MUṢAWWIR

He is the image of the invisible God, the first-born of all creation. Colossians 1:15

The contemporary Arabic word for "photographer" is derived from this word which has several Hebrew parallels in sound, meaning and spelling. Al-Musawwir has close relationships with the previous two names and raises the issue of Adam and the whole human family as created in the "image of God" as found in Genesis 1:27. "Then God formed (Hebrew, *sura*) man from the dust of the ground," reads the companion passage in 2:7. Christians, (alone among the faithful followers of Abraham), by reading the above text of Colossians and similar Bible passages, are convinced that Jesus, the Messiah, fulfills the final portrayal of the image of God.

Jesus is not only the image (Greek, *ikon*) of the invisible God, but is identified in the First Corinthian letter with Adam. Paul cites the creation order:

> The first man Adam became a living being; the last Adam became a life-giving spirit. (15:45)

Earlier he writes, "For as in Adam all die, so also in Christ shall all be made alive" (15:22). Christ, as the image of God, fills those who believe in him with great awe, as the servant is spiritually and majestically placed "in Christ." In order that a follower of Jesus not fall into pride, this lesson in humility is proffered:

> Have this mind among yourselves, which you have in Christ Jesus, who though he was in the form of God,...emptied himself, taking the form of a servant, being born in the likeness of men...He humbled himself and became obedient unto death, even death on the cross. (Phil. 2:5-8)

There is a great amount of discussion among Muslims on what is the image and form of God. A tradition of one of their scholars, Ibn Hanbal, states: "Adam was created in God's image."[1] The discussion stems from the Qur'an's restriction that says, "Compare none with God" (Sura 16:73). This specifically restricts all images and pictures in mosques, and extends to limiting art to geometric designs and calligraphy in Muslim sacred areas.

God's image in Adam did not prevent the creature from being led astray, according to Sura 7 where the two parents confessed, "We have sinned against ourselves" (v. 23) after eating the forbidden fruit. Adam's excuse was a faulty memory of God's command not to taste of the tree, which seemed to be accepted by his Maker in Sura 20:120ff.

The Hebrew Scriptures highlight the creative act of the Maker God and place severe restrictions on forming and fashioning idols. In a single chapter (43), Isaiah links creation and forming with redemption of the kingdom of Israel (v. 1), with God's glorious name (7) and with the people from whom God wants to hear praise (21).

Jeremiah introduces himself as one whom God had known and dedicated to be a prophet "before [Jeremiah] was formed in the womb" (1:5).

Meditation: Your image on Your creation is often clouded over, O my great God. Grant me pardon for losing sight of Your mercy.

Exodus 32:4   Isaiah 45:16   Ecclesiastes 12:1   Hebrews 10:1

---

[1] Cyril Glasse, *The Concise Encyclopedia of Islam* (New York: Harper & Row, 1989), p. 398.

14 The Forgiver   اَلْغَفَّار AL-GHAFFĀR

If my people who are called by my name humble themselves, pray and seek my ways, I will hear from heaven, and will forgive their sin and heal their land.
2 Chronicles 7:14

Beginning with the opening two, Ar-Rahman and Ar-Rahim, and two more to follow, the 99 names hold ample evidence that God's merciful character cannot be understated. The Bible presents the fact that forgiveness and grace are costly. The clothing that Adam first stitches for himself and his wife is made of leaves which provides no satisfactory covering. The Lord substitutes "garments of skins" (Gen. 3:21), and thus institutes the first animal sacrifice for humans who transgress God's holy name. The Qur'an mentions that the first garments were not sufficient, by adding that "piety is the best of dress" (Sura 7:26).

Moses is known for delivering the Torah, the laws of God, to his people. At the first instance of this delivery, he finds the people worshiping the golden calf. In speaking to the people, Moses pleaded to the Merciful One:

> You have sinned a great sin. And now I will go up to the Lord; perhaps I can make atonement (*kafar*) for your sin. (Ex. 32:30)

Moses appears to offer himself as the atoning sacrifice when he adds, "Forgive their sin—if not, blot me out of your book which you have written" (Ex. 32:31f). The sacrifices are introduced for the purpose of at-one-ment for sins that is climaxed in a yearly event called the Day of Atonement. That day is prescribed for the high priest to enter the holy place with the blood of a sacrificed animal as the "sin offering of atonement" (Ex. 30:10).

At the dedication of the first temple, Solomon prays to the Lord, "Forgive the sin of your servants when you teach them the good way" (1 Kings 8:36). The prophet Nehemiah gives instructions at the dedication of the second temple which provide for "sin offerings to make atonement for the people" (10:33). The writer of the Book of Hebrews filled paragraph after paragraph, precept after precept, with the theme of the superiority of Jesus Christ and the greater sacrifice.

> When Christ appeared as a high priest...he entered once for all into the Holy Place, taking not the blood of goats but his own eternal blood, thus securing an eternal redemption. (9:11,12)

In the book of Romans, Paul the apostle provides an outpouring of praise from the servant of God who has been reconciled to God through faith in Jesus Christ: "We have obtained grace and rejoice in our hope of sharing the glory of God" (Rom. 5:2,3).

Meditation: My atoning, seeking God, You are Perfect and Holy in every way; I exalt You for Your daily goodness.

Numbers 8:21   Jeremiah 18:23   Matthew 6:12,13   2 Corinthians 5:21   1 John 1:9

15 The Overcomer, Subduer   اَلْقَهَّارُ AL-QAHHĀR

Give victory to the king, O Lord, answer us when we call. Psalm 20:9

Cairo, the capital of Egypt, was founded by a Shi'a dynasty in 969 A.D. and named after this attribute of God denoting the Victorious One. Today, this exploding metropolis is the largest city on the continent of Africa and a center of education, commerce, and Arab world agencies. For its over sixteen million population there are thousands of mosques and hundreds of churches.

Unlike most of the other names on this list so far, Al-Qahhar has no linguistic equivalent with several Hebrew terms that have similar meanings. The Genesis reference to "a subduer of the earth" (1:28) has a moral note for an "overcomer" in a later prophecy:

> Who is a God like thee, forgiving our sins?...He will again have mercy upon
> us, He will subdue our sins under foot. (Mic. 7:18,19)

King David was constantly at war with his enemies. There was so much blood on his hands that the Lord prevented his building the temple in Jerusalem. Yet God prevailed in bringing David manifold victories against his enemies. Two victories, recorded in 2 Samuel, are short-lived. "So the victory that day was turned into mourning for all the people" (19:2) as they joined their weeping king at the news of the death of David's son Absalom. At the end of David's own life, two battles were celebrated with these words, "The Lord wrought a great victory" (23:10,12). The great leader of the people would soon die.

The choice of words for victory in Psalm 98:1 is instructive as the word turns from an outer struggle to one that deals with salvation (Hebrew, *yashua*): "O sing to the Lord a new song...His right hand and his holy arm have gotten him victory."

Al-Ghazali (died 1111) is one of the most prolific thinkers of the Islamic world and is highly respected even among non-Muslims for his original thoughts in philosophy and theology. In his own short book on the 99 names, he describes the human subduer as one "among men who subdues his enemies. The greatest enemy of man is his soul."[1] A mystic and a philosopher, Ghazali read the gospels several times, according to a Christian tradition.

The Gospel of John speaks clearly about Jesus' own victory, which he passes along to his followers, "Be of good cheer, I have overcome (Greek, *nike*) the world" (16:33). In several references found in 1 Corinthians 15 (54f), Paul identifies the victory as the resurrection. John's first epistle repeats this theme for the servants of God:

> My sons and daughters, you are of God, and are overcomers; for he who is in
> you is greater than he who is in the world. (1 John 4:4)

Meditation: Prepare my own soul to celebrate this eternal victory whereby You have subdued all of Your creation with Your conquest over the last enemy, death.

Isaiah 25:8   1 Corinthians 15:54,55   Hebrews 2:8   1 Peter 5:5   Revelation 15:2

---

[1] Al-Ghazali, *The Ninety-Nine Beautiful Names of God*, trans. David Burrell and Nazih Daher (Cambridge: Islamic Texts Society, 1992), p. 74.

16 The Bestower, Giver of Gifts  AL-WAHHĀB

May God Almighty grant you mercy. Genesis 43:14

The ruling house of Saudi Arabia embraces a very strict brand of Muslim legalisms which are called *Wahhabi*. Native-born Saudis are watched very carefully and non-Muslims are not allowed to worship in any public way; all church buildings are forbidden.

There are many within the kingdom who practice their faith like Joseph in Egypt by serving and worshiping in quiet devotion. "Bestow to the Lord the glory of his name; Worship the Lord in holy array" (Ps. 29:2).

The biblical word is close to this Arabic word which means it has a very ordinary meaning of "give" (Hebrew, *yahab*; Arabic, *wahab*). Joseph, prior to the famine in Egypt where he served as the Pharaoh's chief minister, was asked by the Egyptians, "Give us food." Joseph promised to give them in exchange for their cattle food to take them through the seven years of famine (Gen. 47:15).

Sura 12 describes the life of Joseph with many of the same nuances as found in the longer Genesis narratives (chaps. 37-50). Following the bargaining over the corn and cattle, the Qur'an exclaims that Joseph was firmly established in the land; "mercy is bestowed by God upon whom he wills" (Sura 12:57).

The prophet Daniel favors this word in his Aramaic poetry:
> Blessed be the name of God for ever and ever...Who bestows wisdom to the wise, and knowledge to those who have understanding. (2:20,21)

In successive verses the Almighty God bestows upon Nebuchadnezzar, king of Babylon, "the kingdom" (2:37), and rule over all (38); but according to Daniel's dream all would be the king's loss. Daniel returns the gifts with which the king has favored him with the remark: "Bestow your gifts to another" (5:17).

Jesus, the Anointed One, takes the ordinary word "give" and raises it to the heights of spiritual discernment. On an ordinary day outside the Samaritan city, a woman of meaner moral and ethical values approaches him. "Give me a drink," asks the Christ of the Jews (John 4:7). She is shocked at the request but proceeds to engage Jesus in animated conversation. He responds to her inquiry about his contacts with her, a Samaritan woman:
> If you knew the gift of God, and who it is that is saying to you, 'Give me a drink,' you would have asked him, and he would have given you living water. (4:10)

Shortly after this, Jesus, the Messiah, carries on a similar conversation with some would-be followers who want a miraculous donation of bread.
> Truly, truly, I say to you it was not Moses who gave you the bread from heaven; my Father gives you the true bread from heaven. (John 6:32)

Meditation: Grant me above all things Your daily gifts of life.

Psalm 96:7,8 Hosea 8:3 John 6:65 Romans 5:16, 6:23 James 1:17

17 The Provider   الرَّزَّاق AR-RAZZAQ

But the Provider gives prosperity to his beloved.[1] Psalm 127:2

During his tenure as Pharaoh's chief servant, Joseph uses his sanctified wisdom to heap blessings upon Egypt. At the tender age of thirty, he walks through granaries filled to capacity at his command. His two sons are named Manasseh and Ephraim. The elder signifies, "God has made me forget all of the hardships in all my father's house"; and the younger, "God has made me fruitful in the land of my affliction" (Gen. 41:51,52).

The names of Joseph's sons have the qualities of both pain and mercy. Joseph hears Merciful's voice in accenting forgetfulness and fruitfulness over past brutalization from his brothers and Egyptian master who had him thrown into prison.

> Once God has spoken, twice have I heard this, that power belongs to God and that to thee, O Lord, belongs steadfast love (*hesed*). (Ps. 62:11,12)

God, Ar-Razzaq, is not recognized by that name in the Hebrew Bible, but the image of God as a great Provider prevails in Scripture. During their forty years of wilderness wanderings in the Sinai, God literally rains bread from heaven. Exodus 16 gives the prescribed conditions for the daily, except Sabbath, collections of this marvelous manna. They enter the habitable land of Canaan, a land well provided with "milk and honey" (Deut. 31:20).

The holy God is disappointed in the nation's response to his generous hand, and famine returns to the land. The prophet Amos speaks God's message in biting irony, crying:

> I gave you cleanness of teeth in all your cities, and lack of bread in all your places, yet you did not return/repent." (Amos 4:6)

Moses' words (Deut. 8:3) are repeated by Jesus, the Christ, "Human life does not depend on bread alone" (Matt. 4:4). Yet when Jesus introduces the model prayer, he encourages his kingdom followers to pray for manna for one day: "Give us this day our daily bread" (Matt. 6:11). His servants are to ask for forgiveness much as a wage earner asks for his income, while providing for those who depend upon them for forgiveness. "And forgive us our debts, as we forgive our debtors" (6:12). In the Gospel of John, Jesus declares, "I am the bread of life" (6:48)—the first of several statements that Jesus makes about himself that are introduced by "I am." These will be reviewed in name 94.

Meditation: Do not pass me by without feeding me Your spiritual bread that will nourish me throughout all of my days.

Leviticus 21:6 Isaiah 55:2 John 6:58 1 Corinthians 10:17 2 Thessalonians 3:8

---

[1] The alternative reading of this verse is from Mitchell Dahood, trans., *Psalms* (Garden City, NY: Doubleday, 1970), 3:223.

18   The Opener   اَلْفَتَّاحُ   AL-FATTĀH

O Lord, I am thy servant,...Thou hast opened my bonds. Psalm 116:16

Anyone who serves the Lord with openness finds many examples from Scripture that indicate how the physical body responds both to the Creator and to kindly persons with openness.

In one of his epistles, Paul speaks to his fellow servants about the apostolic self-disclosure: "Our mouth is open to you, Corinthians; our heart is wide" (2 Cor. 6:11). Other parts of the body, human and otherwise, that are open include the hands (Ps. 145:16), eyes (Matt. 9:30), womb (Ex. 13:2), ears (Isa. 50:5), arms (Isa. 52:10). One of the most poignant scenes in all the Bible is the father's embrace of the prodigal son. The waiting parent opens all his heart to the younger son as he lovingly restores the familial bonds (Luke 15:18f).

The Hebrew and the Arabic terms for this name of God are the same. The word is found principally as an action word with both a combative and a peaceful meaning. In the prophecy of Isaiah, the barred gates of Cyrus's enemies will be opened (45:1) while in the Messianic age, the open gates are a symbol of tranquility (60:11). Also, in Isaiah the Servant of the Lord is likened to a lamb "who opened not his mouth" during his hours of oppression and humiliation (53:7).

The Greek Bible impresses upon its readers that the Suffering Servant is none other than Jesus, the Christ. The servant-deacon, Philip, answers the Ethiopian's inquiry concerning this Isaiah text, "Who is this person? Isaiah? or someone else?":

> Then Philip opened his mouth and beginning with this scripture he told them
> the good news of Jesus. (Acts 8:35)

The rich imagery of the final book in the Bible, Revelation of John the Apostle, shows how Al-Fattah, the Opener, has impacted our concept of One who is always open to the pleas of his servants and yet does not force his entry into our lives.

> Lo, I [Jesus] stand at the door and knock; if anyone hears my voice and opens
> the door, I will come in to him and eat with him and he with me. (3:20)

The invitation to enter must come from the inside. There is no bursting of the door from the seeking One on the outside. Kenneth Cragg, a great teacher of Islamics, cites this verse as an example of the freedom that God gives to all persons: "For only the free can be faithful."[1]

Meditation: Open all of my body to Your wonderful, gracious Lordship. I pray for open doors that invitations to Your kingdom can be received.

---

2 Kings 15:17   Psalm 37:14   John 9:10f   Luke 24:32   Revelation 5:2-5

---

[1] Kenneth Cragg, "Christians Among Muslims," *Evangelical Review of Theology* 20, 2 (April 1996): 136.

19 The All-Knowing ٱلْعَلِيمُ AL-'ALĪM

For the Lord knows the way of the righteous, but the way of the wicked will perish. Psalm 1:6

The Hebrew and the Arabic do not share the identical sounds as they do with many of the previous names for God. Both languages are well endowed with words that clearly define "know" and "knowledge" and both agree that the Lord is Omniscient, the perfect Knower. A knower of God first recognizes that God knows him. Our inner and outer thoughts are within the Lord's knowledge. David, the psalmist, proclaims:

> O Lord, you have searched me and known me!...You discern my thoughts from afar. (Ps. 139:1,2)

The Bible speaks of sexual union as knowledge that embodies an intimacy between husband and wife. "Adam knew his wife Eve" (Gen. 4:1). Prior to this knowledge there was a knowledge of "good and evil" where our original parents assumed a godly character of comprehending right from wrong (Gen. 3:7,22). Each human generation seems to forget their divine Knower despite all clues and admonitions to know personally the All-Knowing.

Moses, the Law Receptor, is distinguished from his own people as one whom "the Lord knew face to face" (Deut. 34:10). His first message to the sons of Israel is "Know the Lord" (Ex. 10:2). The Qur'an and the Bible recognize that Joseph is able to know his brothers on their food-seeking trip to Egypt. Both texts indicate that the brothers did not know him (Gen. 42:8; Sura 12:58).

The English words for "teacher" or "teach" are not structurally related to the words derived from "know" as they are in the biblical languages. "Teach me thy way, O Lord" from Psalm 27:11 can be said, "Cause me to learn thy way." Formal teaching became a part of the worship service led by the temple priests (Lev. 4:1-7). In the waning days of the Kingdom of Israel, the prophet Jeremiah sees the vision of the future where priestly teaching would be radically altered:

> And no longer shall each man teach his neighbor...for they shall all know me, from the least of them to the greatest, says the Lord; for I will forgive their iniquity, and I will remember their sin no more. (Jer. 31:34)

The Epistle of Hebrews forthrightly states that the old covenant and its system of sacrifices are made obsolete by the new teaching established by Jesus, the Messiah (8:10f). Jesus is a master teacher from the start of his three-year public ministry. He teaches in synagogues (Mark 1:21), by the sea (Mark 4:1) and in the temple (John 7:14) from Nazareth to Jerusalem.

The teachings of Jesus eventually become the biblical gospels and are incorporated into the teachings of the apostles, which have become the "doctrine" of Christ (2 John 9) and are now available to all his servants. The final words of the Resurrected One are "go and teach" all nations "what I have commanded you" (Matt. 28:19f).

Meditation: O great Teacher, I want to be a steadfast learner and not blown by every wind but wholly instructed by You.

---

1 Kings 8:36   2 Kings 19:19,27   Psalm 46:10   John 14:26   2 Timothy 2:2

99 Beautiful Names of God

20 The Restrainer, The Binder

He binds up the waters in his thick clouds. Job 26:8

The following six names for God are divided into three pairs of words that in casual reading appear to be opposites. The name Al-Qabid, the Constrictor, is positioned on this list with Al-Basit, the Expander. The next double is the Abaser and the Exalter. The third in this series is Honorer and Dishonorer. The entire list of 99 names has several more matched pairs but none as emphatic as these six names.

In his letter to the Roman believers, the writer Paul faces a dilemma about the place of the Jew and non-Jew in God's ultimate plan of salvation. Without any further attempt to solve the problem which involved extensive thoughts on predestination, law, and grace, Paul simply stated:

> Note then the kindness and the severity of God: severity toward those who have fallen, but God's kindness to you. (Rom. 11:22)

There was no attempt to reconcile these two extremes nor did the writer define the limits of God's kindness and his severity. He admitted that in the nature of God there are these two attributes which highlight the significance of the next six divine names. The names are not opposites but part of the same gracious character. God is totally involved in each of these names—the severe ones and the kind ones. He is not limited, as his human creatures are, to single behaviors at a given time. God is totally within his freedom to be all of these 99 and thousands more within a moment of time.

Al-Qabid implies that God is a constricting or binding force in our universe. A Hebrew word (*qafed*) is found in Isaiah 38:12 where King Hezekiah contemplated his death: "Like a weaver I have bound up my life; it is cut off at the loom." Hezekiah's life was spared at that time. What first appeared to be a death note became a poem celebrating God's mercy.

The prophet Abraham faced a similar crisis at the "binding of Isaac" in Genesis 22. Father and son reached the top of the mountain where Abraham was prepared to sacrifice his son, his gentle son, who was already stretched out and bound on the altar (v. 9). The Lord spared this event from its intended climax. Both Abraham and Isaac passed the test—they experienced the mercy of God by obediently accepting the severity of God.

In his second letter to Timothy, the prisoner Paul encourages the young servant with these comforting words:

> Remember Jesus Christ, risen from the dead...the gospel for which I am suffering and wearing fetters like a criminal. But the word of God is not fettered. Therefore I endure everything for the sake of the elect. (2:8,9)

Meditation: Shrink my baser thoughts to conform to Your gracious will and bind me closer to Your magnificent, ever-merciful self.

Psalm 105:22   2 Kings 17:4   Luke 8:29   2 Corinthians 6:11,12   Revelation 20:2

21 The Expander, The Widener  AL-BĀSIT

He has invited you out of distress into a broad place where there is no cramping.
Job 36:16

Modern-day scientists help us understand our universe as an expanding phenomenon. The earliest records of humans following monotheism reason that the natural world, the heavens, and the seasons also prove an ever-widening cosmos. The name Al-Basit has no linguistic counterpart in the Hebrew, but the concept of an Expander-God is implied from Scripture.

The oldest book of the Bible, Job, where the Lord "spoke out of a whirlwind," asks: "Have you comprehended the expanse of the earth?" (38:18). Long before the so-called European Enlightenment, Job, along with his tent-dwelling, debating companions, identifies the mighty God as One who does "great things beyond understanding" (9:6f):

> Who shakes the earth out of its place...who commands the sun...who seals up the stars...who alone extends the heavens.

Isaiah, writing his prophecies in the 8th century B.C., declares that only God is the One

> Who created the heavens and stretched them out, who spread forth the earth...Who gives breath to the people upon it. (42:5)

The physical universe is not alone in its expansive, broadening qualities. Knowledge is God's gift, as in the prayer of Hannah, the mother of Samuel the prophet: "For the Lord God is a God of knowledge" (1 Sam. 2:3).

Daniel, a wise servant of the Living One, not only seeks knowledge in his own life, he sees knowledge as part of future ages, when "many shall run to and fro, and knowledge shall increase" (Dan. 12:4). A contemporary of Isaiah, the prophet Hosea sees the decline of knowledge of God as a decline in belief in Israel: "There is no faithfulness or kindness, and no knowledge of God in the land" (4:6).

At the beginning of the Messianic age, the father of John the Baptist, Zechariah, pronounces that knowledge and redemption will spread out to the people and that John will "go before the Lord to prepare his ways and make his paths straight" (Isa. 40:30, Mark 1:2,3). Jesus went forth "proclaiming the acceptable year of the Lord," in which he welcomed the poor, the captives, the blind, and "set at liberty those who are oppressed" (Luke 4:18). All of this took place to expand God's power among his people on earth which he called the kingdom of God/heaven. A few of the parables that Jesus told in Matthew 13 refer to the mysterious growth of the kingdom, which was compared to seed on good soil (23), a mustard seed (31) and leaven (33).

Meditation: Do not lessen what You have bounteously given to me. Multiply Your good seeds in my life.

---

2 Chronicles 26:15 Job 9:8 Isaiah 40:22 Mark 1:28 Matthew 28:19

22 The Abaser   اَلْخَافِضُ AL-KHĀFID

He who chastens the nations, does he not chastise? Psalm 94:10

A single reference in the Hebrew Bible to the behemoth monster lowering its tail matches the Arabic word Khafid (Job 40:17). The word is found in the Qur'an with an allusion to a bird lowering its wings (Sura 15:88). Other Hebrew words that were general descriptions of the act of debasing are found for this Arabic name. Debasing and dishonoring are practices not limited to God as the Bible records humankind giving and receiving these severe names.

The Book of Psalms provides powerful images of a deity who answers the prayers of a supplicant asking for vengeance over his enemies. In Psalm 94, God is addressed as the Judge "who will render the proud their deserts" (2). The psalm closes with the warning to the wicked, "The Lord our God will wipe them out" (23). An impressive rebuke that sharply strikes at those who attack the "Lord and his anointed [messiah]" is found in Psalm 2:4,5:

> He who sits in the heavens laughs; the Lord has them in derision. Then he will speak to them in his wrath.

There are personal prayers asking for relief for the depths of inner despair. "You have put me in the lower levels of the Pit, in the regions dark and deep" is the cry of the psalmist in 88:6.

A couple of texts speak of the bowing of bodies or heads as a sign of their low positions and perhaps indicating repentance. "Yes, to him shall all the proud of the earth bow down" (Ps. 22:29). The bowing in another instance is to an undesignated figure but, like the Psalm quotation, it fits well the Servant of the Lord. "The sons of those who oppress you shall come bending low to you" (Isa. 60:14).

The prophet Daniel reports the dethronement of the great King of Babylon. Nebuchadnezzar is deposed and driven into madness for not recognizing God's hand upon him. "He was deposed from his kingly throne and his glory taken from him" (5:20).

The New Covenant established by the coming of the Messiah reaches out in hope to those of lowered or debased conditions. The message of the kingdom to the lepers, the morally unclean, and the disenfranchised Samaritans is a word of acceptance and not rejection. Jesus identifies with all of these when he says, "Take my yoke and learn from me; for I am gentle and lowly in heart" (Matt. 11:29).

What about the servant of God who was debased by the wicked ones? Jesus, the master teacher, offers these consoling words:

> Blessed are you when men hate you, and when they exclude you and revile you and cast out your name as evil...Rejoice in that day...for your reward is great in heaven; for so their fathers did to the prophets. (Luke 6:22,23)

Meditation: Forgive me of my sin of wanting to be a servant in Your kingdom, but not being willing to suffer through the times of lowliness and this world's degradations, O my Sustaining Lord.

Psalm 69:9, 102:8   Job 5:17-19, 19:3   1 Timothy 5:14   Hebrews 12:6,7

23 The Exalter  AR-RĀFI'

The Lord brings low, he also exalts. 1 Samuel 2:7

Hannah's prayer at the dedication of her son Samuel provides the reader a remarkable glimpse of the attributes of God expressed by double names. God is a killer and a giver of life (1 Sam. 2:6) and the Maker of the poor as well as the Maker of the rich (7). For the present name of the Almighty Lord, Ar-Rafi', the Hebrew does not match the Arabic vocalizations but suggests a number of words with similar meanings.

The coupling of this word with the previous word continues in Psalm 75 where the Lord "puts down" one person and "lifts up" another (7). The prophet Ezekiel experiences a downer on one occasion which interestingly comes after he is exalted by the Spirit of God:

> The Spirit lifted me up and took me away, and I went in the bitterness, in the heat of my spirit; the hand of the Lord being strong upon me. (Ezek. 3:14)

Isaiah's portrayal of the servant of the Lord is introduced by these words: "Lo, my servant shall prosper, he shall be exalted and lifted up" (52:13). The narration regarding his humiliation and debasement continues throughout the following chapter that concludes with the servant "numbered with the transgressors" (53:12).

Jesus, as the Messianic Servant of the Lord, shares this with his followers: "As Moses lifted up the serpent so must the Son of Man be lifted up" (John 3:14). Moses' lifting up of the serpent on a crude stick was an act of salvation for the tribes of Israel (Num. 21:9). Jesus' use of this Psalm 8:4 reference to the proper name, Son of Man, shows his strong ties with the previous Scriptures and also that he does not want to alarm those who are still considering his call to be followers.

The Qur'an mentions on two critical occasions that Jesus, Son of Mary, was "raised up" (Arabic, *rafa'a*) by God.

> They [the Jews] did not kill him [Jesus], but God raised him up to Himself—God is Mighty and Wise. (Sura 4:158)

A second text includes a phrase about the eventual death of Jesus:

> God said, "O Jesus, truly I shall cause you to die, and I shall lift you up unto Me. (Sura 3:55)

"Lifting up" means only exaltation and honor as Muslims refuse to recognize the death of Jesus as an historical event or its association with redemption. Jesus' answer to those skeptical about his being lifted up is found in the Gospel of John.

> "When I am lifted up I will draw all men to myself." He said this to show by what death he was to die. (John 12:32,33)

The Arabic Bible translates Philippians 2:9 to read, "God has highly lifted up Jesus and given him a name above all names." The servant of God, the lifter-upper, is admonished by James to "Humble yourself before the Lord and he will exalt you" (4:10).

Meditation: Holy God, forgive me for not recognizing Your Servant when he has been lifted up to die for my sins.

Psalm 110:1,7   Isaiah 40:9   Lamentations 3:41   John 8:28   Mark 1:31

24   The Honorer

Those who honor me, I will honor, and those who despise me I will esteem as nothing.
(1 Samuel 2:30)

The Fifth Commandment expresses the Hebrew ideals of the parent-child relationship: "Honor your father and mother." It also supplies a tangible reward for those who keep this commandment. "Your days will be prolonged and prosperous in the land which the Lord God gives you" (Deut. 5:16, Eph. 6:2). The Hebrew word for "honor" (*kabod*) signifies something concrete and tangible as well, often translated as "weighty." It does not share the Arabic vocalization for Mu'izz but they do have common meanings. The Greek for "honor" comes from a root word identified with a set price or reward.

The phrase "A son honors his father" can be expanded to say, "A son gives weightily for his parents' well-being" (Mal. 1:6). The prophet goes further to complain about the priests who had polluted the altar of the Lord and thereby despised the name of the Lord (1:6,7). Isaiah's poetical text cited the honor that wild beasts—jackals and ostriches—bestow upon the Creator to remind the chosen Israelite people of their lack of honor toward their God (43:20).

The thirteenth-century Christian mystic Meister Eckhart exclaims, "Honor belongs to God." He answers the question, "Who are those who honor God?" with this insightful reply: "Those who have gone wholly out of themselves."[1] God honors the servant in Isaiah who is formed in the womb to gather the people back to their Maker (Isa. 49:5).

The Epistle to the Hebrews uses the name the Son of Man (from Psalm 8:4) to identify Jesus, the Messiah, as the superior being:

> You did make him for a little while lower than the angels, You did crown him with glory and honor, putting everything in subjection under his feet. (Heb. 2:7,8)

During his earthly ministry, Jesus, as the Son of Man, addresses his followers in words recorded in John's gospel:

> If anyone serves me, he must follow me; and where I am, there shall my servant be; if anyone serves me, the Father will honor him. (12:26)

Meditation: I admit with my mind that You are worthy of all honor, O Majestic Lord. Yet my soul is troubled because I fail to honor You at all times.

Psalm 111:3   Job 22:8   Daniel 4:34   Mark 15:43   1 Peter 2:17

---

[1] Edmund Colledge and Bernard McGinn, trans., *Meister Eckhart: The Essential Sermons* (New York: Paulist Press, 1981), p. 185.

99 Beautiful Names of God

25   The Dishonorer   اَلْمُذِلُ   AL-MUZILL

We commend ourselves in every way:...in honor and dishonor. 2 Corinthians 6:4,8

The coupling of this word with the previous name for God ends this series of names with great polarities in human behaviors. In God's wisdom, however, the names are not opposites but part of a divine spectrum that humankind sees in single dimensions only. This name, the Dishonorer, describes the severity of God, according to Romans 11:22. In its original Hebrew and Arabic terminology, there is a common root (*zill*). While the Honorer is identified with the Hebrew word for "heavy," the Hebrew source for Dishonorer is associated with words like lightness, insignificant, worthless.

During Jesus' public ministry, he is often vilified by non-believers who see him as a threat to an entrenched legal-religious system. Once a group accuses him of being a Samaritan and possessing a demon. His answer: "I have not a demon; but I honor my Father, and you dishonor me" (John 8:49). Previously many Samaritans believe in Jesus as the result of a Samaritan woman's testimony (John 4:39). Yet when he returns to his own Galilee area, he is largely ignored, which prompted him to say, "A prophet is not without honor except in his own country" (John 4:44).

The Epistle to the Hebrew believers is written against a backdrop of many Christians from Jewish backgrounds who are wavering in their faith. The letter encourages them to be steadfast. It reminds the readers of a former period when the people of God fell into unbelief:

> Today, when you hear his voice, do not harden your hearts as in the day of testing in the wilderness...Therefore I was provoked with that generation...they have not known my ways. (Heb. 3:7f)

The day of rebellion in the wilderness refers to the idolatrous worship centered around the golden calf. The ornaments of the people were used to construct this idol which is being worshiped as Moses is receiving the tables of the law. God's wrath falls upon the whole assembly and three thousand are killed by the Levites. The dishonoring, light-headed actions of the people are put into a song.

> They made a calf in Horeb and worshiped a molten image. They exchanged the honor of God for the image of an ox that eats grass. They forgot God, their Savior. (Ps. 106:19f)

The people continue to forget and dishonor their Creator, and it follows that God will reject them. The message is always there for God's people: if they repent, their lives will be spared. "If you return, I will restore you. If you speak what is worthwhile and not dishonorable trash, you shall be my mouth" (Jer. 15:19).

Meditation: My life's goal is to live honorably before Your Merciful face. O Lord, honor my holy desires even when I fail.

Deuteronomy 8:19   Isaiah 29:13   Psalm 66:2   Proverbs 31:25   1 Corinthians 4:10

26 The Hearer  AS-SAMĪ'

Lo, the Lord's hand is not shortened, that it cannot save, or his ear dull, that it cannot hear. Isaiah 59:1

This word is common to both Hebrew and Arabic with only the opening consonant in Hebrew pronounced as "sh" rather than the "s". The Biblical writers have no particular difficulties in talking about the Lord God's abilities that deal with human senses. This name for God implies that he hears. The name for Abraham's son from Hagar is Ishmael in our Bible (Gen. 16:11) while the Qur'an identifies him as Ismael (Sura 4:163). Both are rendered "El (God) hears."

The next name of the 99 speaks about God seeing. There are other references that mention God's smelling (Gen. 8:21) and touching (Gen. 32:25) which raises the question about the physical characteristics of a God who dwells beyond all human comparisons.

The Muslim theologians have more difficulties than do biblical theologians with these anthropomorphic references. The Qur'an sets up the problem when it states that "God is not like anything but he alone is all-hearing, all-seeing" (Sura 42:11). The Qur'an itself speaks freely about God sitting on a throne (2:27), having eyes (9:3) and hands (5:69). God's expansive presence throughout his creation allows some to accept his immanence without any doubts. Others, Muslims and non-Muslims, maintain that God is totally separated from his creation. Those who hold this latter view of a transcendent God are more likely involved in formal Islamic studies. Those who see/feel/hear God's presence in natural and supernatural settings are more inclined to be associated with practitioners of folk Islam.

The poetical books, Job, Psalms, and Proverbs, along with the writing Prophets widely use anthropomorphic terms. Job ends his book with the confession, "I had heard of you [Lord] by the hearing of the ear, but now my eye sees you" (Job 42:5). A typical psalm begins with prayer: "Incline your ear to me and save me. Be a rock of refuge, a tower to save me" (Ps. 71:2,3). Daniel prays on behalf of Jerusalem as he faces in that city's direction:

> O my God, incline your ear and hear; open your eyes and behold our desolations, and the city which is called by your name...O Lord, hear; O Lord, forgive. (Dan. 9:18,19)

The Gospel of Matthew records the words of Jesus as he speaks to his contemporaries on the shore of Lake Galilee. For that day, Jesus, Son of Man, addresses the crowd in parables, but at his followers' request he tells them the meaning of the parable about the sower. Jesus quotes the prophets Isaiah (6:9) and Zechariah (7:11):

> You shall indeed hear but never understand...For this people's heart has grown dull, their ears are heavy of hearing, and their eyes, they have closed. (Matt. 13:14,15)

The servants of the High God are to "be doers of the word, and not hearers only" (James 1:22).

Meditation: O Divine Listener, hear my pleas, even those that stick in my throat and cannot be formed into words.

Deuteronomy 31:11   Psalm 5:2   Amos 3:1   Ezekiel 33:31   Romans 10:14   1 John 1:1

99 Beautiful Names of God

27   The All-Seeing

Eye has not seen or ear heard, what God has prepared for those who love him.
1 Corinthians 2:9

Jeremiah uses this word to describe "secret mysteries" (33:3) for a rare appearance of the word in the Hebrew Bible. The most common Arabic and Hebrew words for seeing are not used to define God, the Seer, in this list of 99 names. Al-Basir is paired with God the Hearer which is a complementary relationship where two very active physical, human senses articulate the character of the great God. These two anthropomorphic images extend to God's ears and eyes throughout the Bible.

Muslims depend heavily on the ear-gate in their faith. Mosques are places of worship where prayers and suras from the Qur'an are recited. The art form is limited to Arabic script which is there to communicate the Qur'an and secondly to be enjoyed as visual beauty. The eyes are more likely to be openings for temptation and sins than the ears. The Epistle of 1 John lists the "eyes" (2:16) under the lusts of the flesh without any reference to lust of "ears."

God's eyes are ever on the land of promise "from the beginning of the year to the end of the year" (Deut. 11:12). "His eyes are toward the righteous, and his ears toward their cry" (Ps. 34:15). He keeps his eyes on the Jewish leaders while they are rebuilding the city of Jerusalem (Ezra 5:5). But God's gaze is not limited to pleasant places. During the wicked times when there is no justice in the land, "God saw it and it displeased him" (Isa. 59:15).

David, the prophet, affirms that his eyes will not look on "anything that was base" in Psalm 101:3 and that his eyes are set on the "faithful countrymen in the land" (6). Another psalm reminds any arrogant listener that the Lord does not forget his sin and oppression of the weak; Don't ever think thus: "The Lord has hidden his face, he will never see it" (10:11).

Both the Jewish and Christian scriptures report men and women receiving God's message through visions. These messages are most prevalent during the early days of the Jews in exile, Ezekiel and Daniel, and the days of the early church, the Book of Acts and the Revelation. These non-repeatable visions are considered less valuable than the written word that incorporated these images into the text of the Bible. God tells the prophet Habakkuk, "Write the vision; make it plain upon tablets, so he may run who reads it" (2:2).

On the event marking the feast of Pentecost, Peter stands up in the Jerusalem Temple area and declares that the Spirit of God will be poured out on earth and visions will be part of this new experience (Acts 2:14f). He openly proclaims the resurrected Lord by citing several Hebrew Bible texts (2:16,25,34).

Meditation: I need to hear Your voice and see Your hand at work in my daily life. Help me to trust You more fully by knowing You as the Great God over all my life.

Genesis 1:4   Lamentations 1:11,12   Matthew 4:16   Hebrews 11:1   Revelation 6:1

99 Beautiful Names of God

28   The Judge   اَلْحَكَمُ AL-ḤAKAM

Then hear thou from heaven, and act, and judge thy servants. 2 Chronicles 6:23

Throughout the Hebrew scriptures this name is "Wisdom" which has the same vocalizations as its Arabic cognate. The biblical word for judge is not based upon this word, however, and other common Hebrew words derived from *shafat* are used for both the nouns and verbs for "judge." The step from being a wise person to that of being in charge, as was the case for the judges in Israel, was not always a clearly defined step. In the Greek New Covenant texts, believers are encouraged to withhold judgments (Matt. 7:1) and God the Righteous One will complete the judging of the world on the Last Day (Rev. 20:12).

In his review of their short history, Moses speaks to the people of God about his vision of the future when God will rule the people through the law. "For the Lord will judge his people" (Deut. 32:36). The response is hasty and impossible to put into operation as the Israelite tribal society acts in accordance with Moses' farewell message: "Thus the Lord became king in Jeshurun" (Deut. 33:5).

In a 400-year period following the Israelites' entry into the promised land and before the kingdom of David, several men and one woman, Deborah (Judg. 4:4), occupy the office of judge. This period begins at a time of anarchy and often falls into years of sin and lawlessness. There are some outstanding judges who restrain the wickedness, usually connected with idolatry, that was being introduced into the land. Among the more powerful judges are such men as Gideon and Samuel, who was also a prophet (1 Sam. 7:6).

Samuel meets with the leaders of the people who request a king to replace the ineffective rule of the judges. They demand, "We will have a king over us that we also be like all the nations, and that our king may judge us" (1 Sam. 8:20). David, the second in a line of forty kings in Jerusalem, reigns with "justice and equity" (2 Sam. 8:15). Despite the confidence that David brings to the people, the monarchy is soon corrupted by the introduction of idols into the official religion. David is considered a caliph, vicegerent, in the land (Sura 38:26) and is told to make good judgments in following God's path.

The law of Moses becomes an increasingly internal, ethical standard during the dark days of Israel's steady decline as an independent kingdom. Psalm 119 provides a broad picture of what is happening to the laws, the statutes, commandments, all synonyms for "judgments," as they are personalized by the individual Jewish believer:

> I know, O Lord, that your judgments are right, and that in faithfulness you have afflicted me. (75)

The psalm asks for redemption in its closing verse:

> I have gone astray like a lost sheep; seek your servant, for I do not forget your commandments. (176)

A servant of the good and righteous Judge knows that all human rule is very tentative. Our model is Jesus Christ who "suffered, but did not threaten; but trusted [God] who judges justly" (1 Peter 2:23).

Meditation: Hold me accountable to Your righteous standards, O Most Merciful and Compassionate One. Grant forgiveness when I fail.

---

1 Chronicles 16:33   Psalm 75:7   Isaiah 33:22   John 7:24   1 Corinthians 2:6,7

29 The Just   ٱلْعَدَلُ AL-'ADL

There is no other god besides me, a just God and a Savior. Isaiah 45:21

Justice is one of the anticipated results of a good judge. Throughout the world today, the word for peace, *salam, shalom*, evokes a passionate hope for right relationships between nations and between individuals. In the over fifty nations where Islam is the majority religion, there is desire on all levels of society to be treated fairly and to be protected by a just set of laws. Unfortunately, most Muslims in these same regions live on the margins of equitable justice systems where their leaders and judges are partial in reaching judgments.

The word *'adl* is found half a dozen times in the Qur'an where it speaks of the justice of both God and men (Sura 4:58, 6:115). It is used extensively in the Arabic Bibles where it serves several Hebrew and Greek words. The root of the word is found in the name of a minor town southwest of Bethlehem named Adullam where David found refuge in a cave (1 Sam. 22:1). Cities of refuge were introduced earlier as part of Israel's justice system. The most common Hebrew word for justice, *tsedeq*, is translated into several English words as right, righteousness, and just.

The God of justice is recognized throughout biblical history by Moses, "a God of faithfulness...just and right is he" (Deut. 32:4); by Job, "The Almighty, he is great in power and justice" (37:23); by David, "God is a righteous judge" (Ps. 7:11). Intrinsic to God's just ways is the fact that he is "not partial and takes no bribes" (Deut. 10:17). Twice the apostle Paul seizes upon this description of God to build the case for the disposition of God's justice to all, including the non-Jewish world. Galatians 2:6 places the emphasis on the freedom the servant of God finds in the life of faith in Jesus, while Romans 2:11 considers the fact that all are sinners and that salvation is given to all without discrimination.

The prophet Abraham is commissioned to "do righteousness and justice" (Gen. 18:19), which encompasses his faithful obedience to take his son to the mountain and offer him as a sacrifice (Gen. 22, Gal. 3:6f). Because of this act of faith, along with several other great steps of trust, Abraham is justified, made right, before the Lord (Rom. 4:13f). The Epistle of James, speaking of Abraham as the friend of God, complements the letters of Paul by adding, "a man is justified by works and not solely by faith" (2:24).

A justified person is one declared by God to be righteous who still lives under the guidelines that the prophet Amos commends: "Hate evil, and love good, and establish justice in the gate" (5:15). Many Shi'a Muslims today look forward to a "rightly guided one," a Mahdi, to appear and set up justice at the end of time.

Meditation: My world, my communities cry out for justice. Where are You, O Just One, when their pain from injustice mounts up to heaven?

Psalm 37:28   Isaiah 61:8   Jeremiah 5:1   Matthew 11:19   Acts 13:39   Revelation 19:2

30   The Kind One, The Gentle One    AL-LATIF

Blessed be the Lord for he has wondrously shown kindness to me. Psalm 31:21

The names of God, which describe his attributes, are divided into two broad categories—the Gentle and the Severe. This name designates the first of these categories. There is the traditional saying, "My mercy is prior to My wrath," which is supported by the statement in Romans concerning God's kindness and his severity. "Severity to those who have fallen, but God's kindness to you, provided you continue in his kindness" (11:22). A psalm attributed to David heightens the contrast between the "severity and the gentleness" of God. The Lord's voice is a single sound, but the listener may receive two messages: "Power and steadfast love (*hesed*)" both originate with the Merciful One (Ps. 62:11,12).

The most satisfactory word in Hebrew to describe this name is the word hesed which often takes on meanings in English, where it adds adjectives to become loving kindness, tender mercies, and covenant love. As an attribute of God, hesed extends unlimited mercy toward his creation. His kindness will continue for a thousand generations (Ex. 20:6); the earth is full of his kindness (Ps. 33:5); it is great as the heavens (Ps. 103:11).

Kindness and gentleness, defined as loyalty in deep emotional contacts between men, is apparent in these characters of the Bible: David and Jonathan (1 Sam. 20:15), Absalom and his friend (2 Sam.16:17), and King Jehoiachin of Judah who was a prisoner-guest with the King of Babylon (Jer. 52:32). Any kindness shown to the lowly and needy is recognized in God's eyes. The enemies of Israel surrender "because they heard that the kings of the house of Israel were kind" (1 Kings 20:31). Isaiah's expectations for a future king on David's "throne will be established in steadfast love and on it will sit faithfulness" (16:5).

A number of Greek words do not measure up to the subtle strength of the word hesed of the Hebrew Bible. Gentleness often implies meekness as in this quotation from 1 Peter 2:18:

> Servants, be submissive to your masters with all respect, not only to the kind and gentle but also to the overbearing.

Jesus invites his listeners to follow him and "learn from me" and adds, "I am gentle and lowly in heart" (Matt. 11:29). Paul repeats this same invitation in his letter to the Corinthian believers:

> I, Paul, myself entreat you, by the meekness and gentleness of Christ — I who am humble when face to face with you but bold when I am away. (2 Cor. 10:1)

Earlier in this same letter, the apostle speaks directly to those who are servants of God and commends them to show "kindness, the Holy Spirit, genuine love, truthful speech" (6:6). In the Bible for Arab Christians (*latif*) kindness is found in Galatians 6:22 where Paul lists the fruit of the Spirit.

Meditation: Your thoughts are too mighty for me to comprehend, O my Sustainer. They are too gentle for me to ponder.

---

2 Samuel 22:36   Ruth 1:8   Psalm 130:7   Titus 3:2   Hebrews 2:11   Philippians 4:5

99 Beautiful Names of God

31 The Aware One   اَلْخَبِيْر AL-KHABĪR

Sing to the Lord, bless his name; report his glory among the nations. Psalm 96:2

King David awaits for the news about a great battle when there are two separate messages delivered by couriers. The good news is that David's forces won the battle; the bad news delivered by an unsuspecting Cushite, a foreign courier, is that after the heat of the battle David's beloved son, Absalom, died a tragic death. In the Hebrew Bible, the "tidings" of news whether it be good or bad is *basar*, the Arabic *bashar*, which is delivered by the couriers to David in 2 Samuel 18:20f.

This name for God, the Informed One, or the Watchful One, takes its cue from a number of more recent uses of the term Al-Khabir which do not appear in the biblical languages. It forms the root for a host of modern Arabic terms ranging all the way from a news broadcast, to intelligence organizations, to a school exam. The Bible books 1 and 2 Chronicles are "Reports of the Days"; and in Hebrew, these books are "Acts of the Days."

Chronicles attempts to be a daily report of the people of God; but starting with Adam was too daunting a task, and the priestly authorship tends to the lives of the kings of Israel. This again is selective as the reports of earlier books, 1 and 2 Samuel and the Book of the Kings, had previously covered this ground. The late date of around 400 B.C. for the composition of the Chronicles allows the writers to interpret the earlier events in a unique way. There is strong emphasis upon David's life, but it does not distort the fact that he is a man of great sin as well as a great leader in the Kingdom of Israel.

David receives the news from the prophet Nathan that however great he might become, he would not build the temple in Jerusalem (1 Chron. 17:3f). At another time, during the height of his regal power, he disobeys the Lord by taking a census of the population. Again, David has to withdraw his orders and make public confession of his sins. "Take away the iniquity of thy servant, for I have done very foolishly" (21:8). David's murder of the faithful soldier Uriah in order to consummate a rapturous affair with his wife Bathsheba is reported in 2 Samuel. Nathan, the king's seer, hits David hard with God's own report of the incident of adultery, conspiracy, and homicide:

> "Why have you despised the word of the Lord, to do what is evil in his sight?
> You have smitten Uriah with the sword and have taken his wife to be your
> wife...For you did it secretly; but I will do this thing before all Israel, before all
> the sun." (2 Sam. 12:9,12)

What is reported before all the sun is that David's throne will be in jeopardy but will survive. The second son, Solomon, born to David and his wife Bathsheba, proceeds to build the temple. Chronicles picks up the report with the enthronement of Solomon where the new king is proclaimed a "wise son, endued with discretion and understanding, who will build a temple for the Lord" (2 Chron. 2:12).

Meditation: You are the God of the truth often when it is hurtful.

Psalm 96:2   Proverbs 25:25   Isaiah 53:1   Acts 8:34   Romans 10:15,16

32   The Clement, The Forbearing    AL-ḤALĪM

O Lord, remember me and visit me,...in thy forbearance take me not away.
Jeremiah 15:15

This word has taken an extraordinary route to become a divine name, according to the study of scholar J. W. Sweetman. He claims that the original root of this name is related to disturbances of adolescence that providentially grow into maturity when there is a calming and forbearing behavior. Citing the Qur'an, Sweetman notes that *halim* refers to the emotions of Abraham's son "who was led to the sacrifice under submission to his father and not perturbed by the preparations that his father made."[1] One English translation of the Qur'anic verse translates the word with the phrase describing the son, "reached the age when he could work with him [Abraham]" (Sura 37:100).[2]

The Hebrew as well as the Greek words come from altogether different sources, but the idea of the great Creator of the Cosmos who lives in an abode of holiness, yet forbearing toward his human creatures, is evident throughout the Bible. As one of the Merciful attributes, it animates God as Gracious, who does not merely look down from heaven, safely removed from an unholy world, but the glorious God who actually stoops down to look closer at his fallen creatures (Ps. 113:6). "The poor and needy" are granted positions of honor (vv. 7,8), and a barren woman is given the joy of a home and motherhood (v. 9).

An unnamed prophet of God faces King Amaziah, much like Nathan had earlier faced David, with bad tidings from God. Amaziah had introduced the Edomites' gods into Judah, despite the fact that these gods could not offer help to the recently defeated enemies. The prophet is quickly told to shut his mouth, and the servant of God waits for only a moment then finishes his denunciations of the king's idolatry (2 Chron. 25:14f).

A couple of Greek words also point to the fact that forbearance has both divine and a godly, human character. The apostle Paul speaks of God's forbearance, and combines it with God's kindness that will lead a person to repentance (Rom. 2:4). The apostle states that the sacrifice of Jesus Christ for human redemption was done to show both God's righteousness and "his divine forbearance" (3:25). The Letter to the Ephesians asks Paul's fellow servants to show an attitude of forbearance "to one another in love" (4:2). Paul continues in this vein in his appeal to the readers of Colossians when he lists forbearance along with "compassion, kindness, gentleness and patience" in caring for one another (3:12,13).

Meditation: O Eternal Guardian of my soul, multiply Your divine forbearance throughout every cell of my body.

Isaiah 53:7   Proverbs 25:15   Ezekiel 3:11,27   Acts 8:32,33   2 Corinthians 11:1

---

[1] J. Windrow Sweetman, *Islam and Christian Theology*, part 1, vol. 2 (London: Lutterworth Press, 1947), p. 49.

[2] N. J. Dawood, trans., *The Koran* (London: Penguin Books, 1990), p. 315. Hereafter cited as The Koran.

99 Beautiful Names of God

33   The Mighty One   الْعَظِيمُ   AL-'AZIM

So I have looked upon thee in thy sanctuary beholding thy might and glory. Psalm 63:2

There is no shortage of words in the Bible that recall God's strength, power, might, greatness, etc. The root of the Hebrew word is from the word for "bone" which is pronounced the same in both Hebrew and Arabic. When *'azoum* is found in the Bible, it frequently speaks of mighty nations (Gen. 18:18 and Deut. 4:38) and other natural phenomena, such as many locusts (Jonah 1:6) and mighty waters (Isa. 8:7).

The Bible uses the comparative adjective "greater" to express something mightier, as found in this confession of Jethro, Moses' father-in-law:

> Now I know that the Lord is greater than all gods because he has delivered the
> people from under the hand of the Egyptians. (Ex. 18:11)

Jesus finds this metaphor useful in speaking about his redemptive mission to the world. He answers questions from the Pharisees, the legal masters of his day, by referring to himself, "A greater than Jonah is here" (Matt. 12:41). He follows that remark with another more marvelous, "A mightier than Solomon is here" (v. 42). Later, he spoke to his followers, "Truly, truly, I say to you a servant is not greater than his master" (John 13:16).

In the sura reporting Abraham's sacrifice of his tender son,[1] the Qur'an announces, "We ransomed him with a mighty sacrifice" (37:107). Several Muslim commentators state that the ram which is provided for God is the mighty sacrifice substitute for the son. "Abraham took the ram and offered it up as a burnt offering instead of his son" (Gen. 22:13).

The sacrificial death of the suffering servant has played an important role for Christians in understanding the substitutionary death of Jesus the Messiah. The four Gospels record the "mighty sacrifice" of Jesus Christ, and the Epistles build upon the faith that grows out of the strong affirmations that Jesus did die on the cross for sinners. Throughout the Book of Hebrews, the writer develops this theme: Jesus is greater than angels (1:13), than Moses (3:3), and greater than all the previous sacrificial systems (9:11-14). The laws of God themselves cannot measure up to the mighty death of Jesus:

> But when Christ had offered for all time a single sacrifice for sins, he sat down
> at the right hand of God. (Heb. 10:12)

Meditation: O Mighty God, help Your servant to reflect Your steady hand and magnificent heart toward all of Your creation.

Job 17:9   Psalm 48:1   1 Chronicles 21:8   1 John 3:20   1 Corinthians 1:25, 10:22

---

[1] Muslims have held that Ishmael was the elder son and therefore the intended son of the sacrifice. The mystic thinker Ibn Arabi (d. 1325) was among many early Muslim scholars who admitted that Isaac was the son led to the altar of sacrifice. Refer to *The Bezels of Wisdom* (New York: Paulist Press, 1980), p. 99.

34 Great Forgiver ٱلْغَفُورُ AL-GHAFŪR

To the Lord our God belong mercy and forgiveness; because we have rebelled against him, and have not obeyed...his laws which he set before us by his servants the prophets. Daniel 9:9,10

Al-Ghafur, another name that discloses the intense emotion of God's forgiveness, is closely akin to name 14, Al-Ghaffar. Both are parallel to the Hebrew which provides us with the ordinary English word for cover. Ar-Rahman and Ar-Rahim head this current list of names, indicating that God's forgiveness and mercy are continually bestowed upon humankind.

Near the close of the Hebrew Bible, the prophet Ezra recites the great acts of salvation that the Creator had performed over the 600 years of Israelite history, beginning with the calling of Abraham, to the end of the Babylonian captivity. The prophet-preacher punctuates his long sermon with references to both the people's corporate sins and God's generous display of forgiveness (Neh. 9:6f). On one hand are the constricting powers of wickedness and on the other is the expanding goodness that opens with Abraham's faithfulness (v. 8) and the redemption of the people at the Red Sea exodus (10).

In the next forty years, when the Sustaining God hand-fed them, the people's responses were startling: "But our fathers acted presumptuously and stiffened their neck" (Neh. 9:16). Ezra addresses the Lord, "But you are a God ready to forgive" (17) and "You did not forsake them in the wilderness" (19). In the land of promise, they fill and delight themselves (25) while they neglect "the law of God and killed God's prophets...and they committed great blasphemies" (26). The restricting and expansive movements of a people with their Lord continue in a dance that Ezra swore would not end in a tragedy. That chapter closes with the leaders of the people signing and sealing a covenant which binds them by oath "to walk in God's law which was given by Moses the servant of God" (10:29).

Jesus' Messianic ministry opens five centuries after Ezra's warnings to the people. He has to overcome several attempts to discredit his privilege to be called the Son of Man, a subtle title that will not distract his true followers. His acts to heal and forgive sins are even more unwelcome (Matt. 9:2f). The latter claim will lead eventually to Jesus' death as a blasphemer (Matt. 26:65).

The Qur'an specifically names these prophets as needing forgiveness: David (Sura 38:2), Jonah (21:87), Noah (71:2) and Abraham (14:41). Muhammad, the Arab apostle himself, was promised forgiveness for past and future sins (48:2).

The apostles' message to the Jews of Jerusalem is that Jesus is the "exalted leader and savior to give repentance and forgiveness of sins" (Acts 5:31). Paul repeats this theme in a sermon to non-Jews in Acts 17:30.

Meditation: O Omnipotent One, forgive my undulating, feverish ways, and I pray that You help me to see Your mighty patience in my ups and downs.

Leviticus 4:20,26   1 Kings 4:36   Psalm 51:1,2   Ephesians. 1:7   1 John 1:9

35 The Thankful One   ٱلشَّكُورُ ASH-SHAKŪR

We give thanks to thee, Lord God Almighty. Revelation 11:17

The divine thankfulness is a response to the thanks that the created world offers freely to God. The biblical languages do not offer much to support the idea that the Almighty expresses thanks to his creation for human acts of righteousness and kindness. The word *sakar* in Hebrew is associated with terms such as hire, wages and reward, which are allied to experiences and persons worthy of praise and thanks.

The common Hebrew word for thanks is found in the name Judah, and the writings of Paul in Greek help locate a couple instances where God offers thanks. In Romans 2:29, the apostle defines a Jew as one who has an inner, spiritual experience, who received thanks, *yudah*, from God not from men. The Lord will also become the Thanksgiver at the day of judgment when all things will be opened. "Then every man will receive his commendation from God" (1 Cor. 4:5).

God is the object of thanks throughout the Hebrew text. God giving thanks is rare, and that is due to linguistic as well as religious questions like, "Who is the great Lord going to thank or make confession to?" The Hebrew word *yudah* also means confession, as in confession of sins. "Ezra prayed and made confession, weeping and casting himself down" (Ezra 10:1).

The word for bless, *barak*, in both Hebrew and Arabic, has a more reciprocal capacity whereby God becomes both the subject and object of blessing; likewise, humans also can receive from and give blessings to God. At the meeting of Abraham with Melchizedek, the latter offers this prayer:

> Blessed be Abram by God Most High, Maker of heaven and earth; and blessed
> be God Most High who has delivered your enemies into your hand. (Gen.
> 14:19,20)

There are blessings all around — the two men of God with their High God esteeming, honoring, thanking each other. After Moses receives the law, the Lord instructs the people to build an altar where his name will be honored and where he will bless the people (Ex. 20:24). While God blessing men is neither grammatically nor religiously the same as God thanking men, the two thoughts are based upon positive interactions between two beings, where one or both are in the other's obligation. The English translator of the Qur'an embellishes Ash-Shukur to read, "ever responsive to gratitude" (Sura 35:30).[1]

Praises to God flourish throughout the Holy Scriptures. Nowhere is this more evident than in the psalms written for the temple services. "I will offer to you the sacrifice of thanksgiving" (Ps. 116:17) is typical of many other sacred songs.

Meditation: Your thankfulness toward me is seen in every minutia of my existence. My desire is to thank You for Your all-encompassing care.

Genesis 49:8   2 Samuel 22:50   Psalm 106:1   Amos 4:5   Luke 22:19   Colossians 1:3

---

[1] Muhammad Asad, trans., *The Message of the Qur'an* (Gibraltar: Dar Al-Andalus, 1984), p. 670.

36 The Most High اَلْعَلِيُّ AL-'ALĪ

For the shields of the earth belong to God; he is highly exalted. Psalm 47:9

There is no end to God's presence; finding suitable words to define the place of God's abode leaves the human mind exhausted. For the biblical writers, God is far above all of his creation. This name for God is found in both Hebrew and Aramaic, with close affinities in sound and meanings to the Arabic.

The skies or the heavens are described as the place where the Lofty One occupies a superior position over his creation.

> Look down from your holy habitation, from heaven, and bless your people Israel. (Deut. 26:15)

The prophet Job asks, "Is not God high in the heavens? See the highest stars, how lofty they are!" (22:12). God assumes the position of being "up" there, and his mighty name attests to his separation, his holiness, each defined by height. "Your righteousness, O God, reaches the high heavens" (Ps. 71:2). Jeremiah's perspective of God's exalted place is colored by his vision of a heavenly temple, "a glorious throne set on high from the beginning" (17:12). The prophet Isaiah's vision comes to him as a young man when he "saw the Lord sitting upon a throne, high and lifted up" (6:1).

In his later writings, Isaiah hears the voice of the Merciful say:

> I dwell in a high and holy place, and also with him who is of a contrite and humble spirit, to revive the spirit of the humble, and the heart of the contrite. (57:15)

A contemporary of Isaiah, the prophet Micah, sees the splendor of his God but realizes that this same God walks with the lowly servants.

> With what shall I come before the Lord, and bow down myself before God on high?...He has shown you, O man, what is good;...to do justice, and to love kindness (*hesed*), and to walk humbly with your God. (Mic. 6:6,8)

In the new Messianic era, a similar adoration of God's profound presence can be noted. The angel Gabriel announces to Mary the mother of Jesus that her "son will be great, the Son of the Most High" (Luke 1:32). Zechariah speaks prophetically at the circumcision of his son, John, who will be called "the prophet of the Most High" (Luke 1:76). During the public ministry of Jesus Christ, a demon-possessed man encounters Jesus and "worshiped" him by addressing him as "Son of the Most High God" (Mark 5:6,7).

Outside the temple area, the deacon Stephen, who becomes the first martyr, enrages his listeners: "The Most High does not dwell in houses made with hands" (Acts 7:47). Paul and his traveling companions are followed by a slave woman who is possessed by a spirit of divination. She shouts out, "These men are servants of the Most High God, who proclaim to you the way of salvation" (Acts 16:17).

Meditation: The natural world of the heavens and the deep seas testify of Your depths and loftiness, O Most High God.

Genesis 14:18,19,20   Psalm 99:2   Daniel 7:18,22   Romans 12:16   Hebrews 7:1

37 The Great, The Eminent One   الكَبِير AL-KABĪR

The Almighty—we cannot find him; he is great in power and justice. Job 37:23

A simple form of this name appears as number 10 on this list of names. Al-Mutakabbir is God's majestic greatness in contrast to the human pretense at greatness, which is interpreted as pride and arrogance. Although there are several other biblical words that are relevant to this Arabic term, the most widely used in the Hebrew Bible is *gadol*. It may describe both God and man as well as other animate and inanimate subjects. God communicates greatness about himself, and the Bible is cognizant that the creation and the creatures may reflect this attribute.

Nowhere is this complementary statement of human greatness more concentrated than in the Bible references to John the Baptizer. John's father, Zechariah, is told by an angel that John will be great (Luke 1:15). At the opening of the public ministry of Jesus Christ, John witnesses of the Greater One: "After me comes a man who ranks before me" (John 1:30). Just before his death by beheading, John speaks of his loyalty to the Christ, "He must increase, but I must decrease" (3:30).

Jesus renders his high praises for John but reserves his highest praises for something greater than John.

> I tell you, among those born of women, none is greater than John; yet he who is least in the kingdom of God is greater than he. (Luke 7:28)

Psalm 99 is typical of several psalms that glorify the "enthronement" of the Lord: "The Lord is great in Zion...Let the people praise your great name" (2,3). The idea of a High Divine Being sitting on a heavenly throne does not disturb the people of God because they realize that their Sovereign King is greater than all other kings, gods, and even their highest thoughts. "Allah Akbar" is not just a hollow phrase for jubilant Muslims around the world. "God is greater..." leaves unsaid what he is compared to, as nothing can be compared/contrasted to God (Sura 16:73).

The prophet Ezra contrasts God with the former times. All of the hardships of the kings, the prophets, all the people are diminished because, "Our God is the great and mighty one" (Neh. 9:32). A great fish is prepared for the reluctant prophet Jonah to force him to go to the great city of Nineveh (Jonah 1:17). There the prophet, still unable to overcome his pride, cries out to the Great God: "I know that you are gracious and merciful (*rahum*) and abounding in steadfast love (*hesed*)" (4:2).

When Jesus begins to proclaim the good news of the gospel, he uses the story of Jonah to announce in enigmatic, parabolic expressions that he will be buried in the earth for "three days and three nights" (Matt. 12:40). He concludes his words with an appeal for his listeners to repent like the Ninevites repented at the preaching of Jonah and adds, "something greater than Jonah is here" (12:41).

Meditation: You are greater than my fear. My heart does not condemn me for Your heart is stronger than all the world.

Deuteronomy 10:17 Job 34:37 Hebrews 11:26 1 John 3:20

38 The Preserver  AL-HAFIZ

Behold, He who keeps Israel will neither slumber nor sleep. Psalm 121:4

God, as the Preserver and Keeper, provides a great help to the believer (*al-mu'min*) who is the subject of number 7 in this list of the beautiful names of God. The Arabic and Hebrew words are practically identical, with the exception that the Hebrew Bible emphasizes the attributes of delight and pleasure, which are tied to the words of keeping and holding on. The Arabic has not retained the concepts of delight and pleasure, yet *hafiz* has broad modern-day usage.

The pleasure/preserver motif is applicable in many situations in the Hebrew text. Prior to entry into the land of promise, Joshua, encouraged by what he sees, reports: "If the Lord delights/preserves us, he will bring us into the land" (Num. 14:8). God's transcendent behavior, his glory, is marvelously contrasted with the glories of the wise man, the mighty, the rich man, in this passage from Jeremiah:

> But let him who glories know this...I am the Lord who practices steadfast love (*hesed*), justice and righteousness in the earth; for in these things I delight/preserve, says the Lord. (9:24)

Prior to the coming of the Messiah, the Lord's messenger is expected to appear in Jerusalem. Malachi, the final Hebrew writing prophet, proclaims that this messenger is one in whom the Lord delights/preserves (3:1). Queen Esther's King Ahasuerus finds delight in his servant Haman at first, but Haman later loses the king's favor for conspiracies against the Jews (Est. 6:6f). The Jews had been targeted for annihilation by Haman who is plotting against the people of God, because they "do not keep the king's laws" (3:8).

The most common word describing the keeping and preserving of God's commandments is the Hebrew word *shamar*. In the lengthy poetry of Psalm 119 the "keeping" is linked with God's statutes (v. 8), law (44), words (57), precepts (134), testimonies (168). The prophet Nehemiah's faith in the preserving power of God is contingent upon the people's keeping faith with God's law.

> O Lord God of heaven, the great and terrible who keeps covenant...with those who love him and keep his commandments, let thy ear be attentive to hear the prayer of thy servant. (Neh. 1:5)

In the Gospel of John are numerous sayings of Jesus about keeping his words: "If you love me, keep my commandments" (14:15). "Truly, truly, if anyone keeps my word, he will never see death" (8:51). Later the Elder John admonishes the new generations of God's servants with these words, "By this we know that we love the children of God, when we keep his commandments" (1 John 5:2).

Meditation: You are the One who keeps me on the right path. By Your watching eye and Your gentle voice, You do not abandon me in the rough ways.

Genesis 2:15   1 Kings 8:23,24   Psalm 111:2   Proverbs 7:1   2 Timothy 1:12

39 The Nourisher  AL-MUQĪT

He gives to the beasts their food, and to the young ravens which cry.
Psalm 147:9

Psalm 23 is included in the world's most popular literature because it speaks to all who desire safekeeping during times of stress. For those seeking solace, the psalm's beautiful, simple verse and pastoral setting are there to lift one up to an embracing Lord. The shepherding God is a Nourisher and Sustainer. The present Arabic name for God is not found in the Hebrew, but the image of the nourishing shepherd, the pastor, is at home throughout the Bible.

From Genesis (30:31) to Revelation (7:17) shepherds feed their herds of sheep, goats, camels, with the good food provided by the Great Creator. Outstanding leaders are honored to be called shepherds, as was the case for David (2 Sam. 5:2) and the Persian monarch Cyrus (Isa. 44:28). Both of these men were anointed, called to be leaders by the Lord; and like the sheep in Psalm 23:5, their heads were ritually smeared with oil.

The great writing prophets of the Hebrew Bible, Isaiah, Jeremiah, and Ezekiel, vividly describe the ministry of shepherding the wandering flocks of Israel. Isaiah speaks of the Lord:

> He will feed his flock like a shepherd, he will gather the lambs in his arms, he
> will carry them in his bosom. (40:11)

Jeremiah's visions of a return of the people as sheep to graze on the former pastures provide hope for the people while they are in captivity (50:19). Ezekiel devotes several paragraphs to the pastor-shepherd, who is identified as the Lord God. "Lo, I, myself, will search for my sheep, and will seek them out" (34:11). The prophet envisions the day when God acts:

> I will set up over them one shepherd, my servant David, and he shall nourish
> them; he shall feed them and be their shepherd. (34:23)

The "good shepherd" is a compelling teaching motif for Jesus, the Messiah. Often he draws upon the Hebrew text like this from Ezekiel 34. The following are Jesus' words based upon Ezekiel:

> I am the good shepherd...and I will lay down my life for the sheep...I have
> other sheep, that are not of this fold; I must bring them also...So there shall be
> one flock, one shepherd. (John 10:14,15,16)

With the prophets, Jesus recognizes that his mission to the world is to bring salvation. He is responding to the prayers of Psalm 28:9: "O save your people...be their shepherd, and carry them for ever." When Jesus tells the story of a single lost sheep from a flock of a hundred (Matt. 12:11), he heard the voice of the one sheep cry from Psalm 119, "I have gone astray like a lost sheep" (176).

The pastoral-servant ministry of a flock is passed to the ever-failing disciple, Peter, by the resurrected Messiah, when he repeatedly tells the apostle to "feed," "tend," nourish "my lambs and my sheep" (John 21:15f).

Meditation: Tender Shepherd of my soul, nourish me and sustain me.

---

1 Samuel 17:5   Ezekiel 34:14   Psalm 23   Acts 20:28   1 Peter 5:2   1 Corinthians 9:7

40 The Reckoner  AL-HASĪB

Abraham believed the Lord; and he reckoned it to him as righteousness.
Genesis 15:6

Arab accountants are professionally identified with this name for God. The root word comes from a common Arabic-Hebrew source, and the differences even today are minimal. God is introduced early to Abraham as a "Reckoner," who will count Abraham as a righteous one, based upon Abraham's and God's faith in one another (Gen. 15:6).

In the New Covenant era, Paul the apostle constructs his treatise of salvation through Jesus Christ upon this and other Hebrew texts. The apostle uses a Greek word that is related to our English word "logic," which forms the basis of his argument and helps define the word "reckon" to mean take into account, consider, ponder. "Abraham believed God, it was looked upon as righteousness" (Rom. 4:3). Abraham is accounted righteous, not for any good works that he is storing up to please God, but strictly for his faith in the Merciful, Graceful One. David is likewise pronounced "righteous apart from works," according to Psalm 32:1,2, which Paul cites in his letter to the Romans (4:7,8).

Joseph's brothers reckon that they are doing ill to Joseph when they sell him to slave traders on their way to Egypt. But according to Joseph's reckoning, God turns all of these experiences for good "to bring about that many people should be kept alive" (Gen. 50:20). God's accounting system lifts up the heart of the psalmist when he cries, "As for me, I am poor and needy; but the Lord takes thought for me" (Ps. 40:17).

The human capacity to reckon is worded in a positive way as "esteeming" and in the negative sense as "plotting." In the latter, Esther's people are the victims of evil plotters who want to see the Jews destroyed, according to Esther 9:24. When Isaiah mentioned the threat of the invading armies, he reports that the Medes have no esteem for gold or silver usually used to bribe a general (Isa. 13:17). The Suffering Servant of Isaiah 53 is esteemed as a "man of sorrows and acquainted with grief" (3).

The Gospel of Luke informs us that Jesus as the Servant will be "reckoned with sinners" as his death draws near. Luke 22:37 cites Isaiah 53:12 where it says, "He was numbered with transgressors."

A casual and even a thorough understanding of the gospel will find Paul's counting system highly unusual, even uncomfortable. The servant Paul reviews his former life as a zealot for God and his righteousness even to the point of becoming a persecutor of the church. He looks at his new reckonings:

> But whatever gain I had, I counted as loss for the sake of Christ. Indeed I count everything as loss because of the surpassing worth of knowing Christ Jesus my Lord. For his sake I have suffered the loss of all things, and count it as refuse that I may gain Christ. (Phil. 3:7,8)

Meditation: Amen, Great God, I am myself a loss without You.

---

1 Chronicles 5:1   Job 13:24   Psalm 44:22   Galatians 3:6   1 Timothy 1:12, 6:1

41   The Sublime

 AL-JALĪL

Deep calls to deep...all thy waves and thy billows have gone over me. Psalm 42:7

There is a traditional saying that circulates among Muslims before a child is given a name. Supposedly on judgment day when one is called by his or her name, the name itself may help one find favor at this critical time.[1] Jalil is one of those beautiful names of God that has auspicious meanings in this world and the next! The Hebrew word, with closely matching sounds, has variant meanings from the Arabic "sublime" but it poignantly suggests natural and poetic beauty.

One of the Hebrew definitions for this word is "on account of" as it is used in the story of Joseph. The house of the Egyptian where he serves as a servant is singularly blessed "on account of Joseph" (Gen. 39:5). Jeremiah recalls some of the horror that is falling on the people of Israel "on account of" the wicked king Manasseh, son of Hezekiah (15:4).

Other Hebrew words related to Jalil are pleasant sounding for rolling, as in "the heavens roll up like a scroll" (Isa. 34:4), "waves and billows" (Ps. 42:7) and round shaped objects like bowls and the Sea of Galilee, which comes directly from *galil*. Other expressions of God's beauty that use alternative words include these two from Psalms: "Out of Zion, the perfection of beauty, God shines forth" (50:2), and "Strength and beauty are in his sanctuary" (96:6). Another poet celebrates the sublimity of both creation and eternity, "He has made everything beautiful in its time; also he has put eternity into men's minds" (Eccl. 3:11).

The poetry of the Hebrew Bible has a simple and natural quality that allows it to weave deep philosophical thoughts into household language through poems, proverbs and even love stories. As the poet Solomon the Wise grows older he recognizes that pleasure apart from fearing God is empty. He closes his thoughts with this word:

> For God will bring every deed into judgment, with every secret thing, whether good or evil. (Eccl. 12:14)

The poetry of the Song of Solomon tells an alluring story of human romance that mystics have interpreted as divine messages hidden in earthy language. The sublime may be extracted from a single poem that glorifies and magnifies love: "I am my beloved's and his desire is for me" (Song 7:10).

The best poetry in the Greek Bible makes no pretension of being a poem. Its author, Paul, begins by saying: If I speak in the sublime language of angels, prophets, and understand all mysteries "but have not love then I gain nothing" (1 Cor. 13:1-3). The poet-apostle goes on to praise the virtues of active *agape*, spiritual love. Love will abide longer than faith and hope (13).

Meditation: Set a word in my lips, and praise in my throat as You provide melodies for my heart to sing.

Psalm 84:1,2   Isaiah 25:2   Daniel 5:18,19   Ecclesiastes 1:12-15   1 Corinthians 13

---

[1] Annemarie Schimmel, *Islamic Names* (Edinburgh: University Press, 1989), p. 14.

42 The Bountiful One  AL-KARĪM

Deal bountifully with thy servant, that I may live and observe thy word.
Psalm 119:17

This name for God is also a beautiful name for a son or daughter. It combines with Al-Jalil to form the 85th name on this list of 99 names. The Hebrew and Arabic linkage is not overt as the Bible limited the use of this word to vineyards, fruit and fertile lands. Mount Carmel might have been originally Mount Carmel after the fertility gods in that region. Its present name ends with God's name, El, indicating that the prophet Elijah won a great victory over the gods and goddesses of Baal at this mountain in northern Israel (1 Kings 18:19f).

The Greek Bible also uses agricultural and natural terms to describe the inner, spiritual life. Jesus speaks of "good" and "bad" fruit from good and bad trees (Matt. 12:33), good and poor crops and soils (13:24f), as well as harvests (9:38). Paul employs the terms fruit of the Spirit (Gal. 5:22), fruit of righteousness and the fruit of the flesh (Phil. 1:11). The mental picture of a Generous God providing good fruit is strengthened when the seed and faith are multiplied.

> He who supplies seed to the sower and bread for food will supply and multiply your resources and increase the harvest of your righteousness. (2 Cor. 9:10)

"Be fruitful and multiply" is the command from the Bountiful One to all creatures (Gen. 1:22). Repeated several times in the first chapters of Genesis, this command to bear fruit is especially evident in God's word to the prophet Abraham when he tells him his seed will be multiplied over the face of the earth. Ishmael is included in this promise as he will multiply "exceedingly" as the father of twelve princes (17:20). Following the intended sacrifice of Isaac, the Lord says to Abraham:

> I will indeed bless you, and I will multiply your descendants as the stars of heaven and as the sand which is on the seashore. (22:17)

The multiplication continues for the people of God through the years of Egyptian bondage and the successive Exodus years. Moses reviews God's generous mercy, which begins with the covenant love, *hesed*. "He will love you, bless you, and multiply you; he will also bless the fruit of your body" (Deut. 7:13). The seed of David will not die but will live throughout all generations: "I will multiply the descendants of David my servant, and the Levitical priests who serve me" (Jer. 33:22).

"Peace be multiplied" is the message that went out to all nations and languages from King Nebuchadnezzar, according to Daniel 4:1. The letters of 1 and 2 Peter and Jude all include the salutation that greets their readers with "grace and peace be multiplied" in their opening second verses. The early servants of the church are all encouraged by the reports in Acts 6:1 and 7 that the number of disciples is multiplying.

Meditation: You are generous, O my Maker. The creation reflects that bountiful care which I can tenderly cultivate or carelessly destroy.

Exodus 1:1,18,20   Psalm 13:6, 119:7   Acts 6:1   2 Corinthians 9:6   Hebrews 6:14

43   The Jealous Guardian

For I the Lord thy God am a jealous God. Exodus 20:5

God's watchful care over his creation includes the emotion of jealousy and has specific similarities to a husband's devotion to his wife. "For jealousy makes a husband furious" (Prov. 6:34) sets in motion a chain of warnings that the commandment of Exodus 20 refers to as "visiting the sins of the fathers to the third and fourth generation" (v. 5). God's anger at the tribes of Israel during their wilderness wanderings is directed against those who are involved in worshiping foreign gods. The high priest, Aaron, intercedes one time and is able to turn aside the anger of God, who declares that he would have "consumed them all in my jealousy" (Num. 25:11).

This name is based upon a rare use of the word for jealous, which also means covetous. The Arabic Bible uses the conventional word for jealousy in its translation of Exodus 20:5, "For I the Lord thy God am a jealous God."

During the darkest days of the Israelite monarchy, the powerful yet all-merciful God raises up the prophet Elijah who on Mount Carmel humiliates hundreds of the god Baal's prophets. The details of this victory are recorded in 1 Kings 18, which the Qur'an alludes to in Sura 37. Elijah (Elias in Arabic) taunts the Baal worshipers, "Will you call upon Baal and forsake God, the best of all creators?" (2:123). Like much of the Qur'anic verses covering characters and events from the Bible, this passage assumes that its listeners know the narratives and characters of the Bible.

A short time after the Mount Carmel victory over the gods and goddesses of the Canaanites, Elijah cries out, not in joy, but in despair:

> I am very jealous for the Lord, the God of hosts, for the people of Israel have forsaken thy covenant...slain the prophets with the sword, and I even I am left, and they seek my life. (1 Kings 19:14)

The Lord offers assurance that Elijah is not alone in his stand against polytheism, as there were 7000 "who did not bow down and kiss Baal" (19:18).

The prophet Zechariah clearly describes God's character in guarding his city and people, "I am exceedingly jealous for Jerusalem and for Zion" (1:14). These words follow their Babylonian captivity when the Jews try to rebuild their city near Mount Zion, the sacred hill of David. After their capture, the city and the nation are rid of false gods, but they are not free from other sins. These are exposed by the teaching of Jesus, who offers Jerusalem the message of repentance (Luke 13:4,5).

Meditation: Teach Your servant Your perfect ways, including Your righteous jealousy guarding me.

Psalm 78:58   Isaiah 42:13   Zechariah 8:2   Romans 10:19   2 Corinthians 11:2

44 The Responsive One  AL-MUJĪB

Answer me, O Lord, answer me, that this people may know that thou, O Lord, art God, and that thou has turned their hearts. 1 Kings 18:37

God answers Elijah's prayer by pouring fire from heaven and consuming Elijah's thoroughly-prepared sacrifice at Mount Carmel. The false prophets are seized and killed at the brook Kishon. God's answers are not always this dramatic as the prophet of God hides out in a cave for a period of inner reflection. His cries of remorse and pain, directed to a listening God, evoke a remarkable response. The Lord sends natural events: a strong wind that breaks rocks and splits mountains, then an earthquake and a fire. But the Lord is not heard in any of these. After the fire "he sent a still small voice" (1 Kings 19:12). God's righteous prophet hears the answer.

The Hebrew Bible has both God and his servants answering one another, but with words that do not include this Arabic word for "answer." It does appear in modern Arabic literary and oral communications. Al-Mujib, the Answering One, has hundreds of conversations with his creatures throughout Scripture, including the friendly discussion with an unnamed person in the opening chapters of Genesis, "Let us make man in our own image, after our likeness" (1:26). God gives Adam the gift of speech when he asks him to name the beasts of the field and of the skies (2:19).

The Book of Job contains some of the best writing in the Hebrew Bible, including dramatic dialogues between Job and his friends. The first dialogues, however, are between God and Satan. When the Lord asks, "Whence have you come?" Satan answers, "From going to and fro on the earth" (Job 1:7). Job's friends, with various attitudes, enter the conversations that follow the Lord's granting Satan power over Job, except for his life (1:12).

The wise counselors take their time in answering Job's cries for understanding and for death. He directs his answer to Bildad with another question about God's justice, "But how can a man be just before God?" (9:2). Job's faith wavers, but in the end he provides his own confident answer: "For I know that my Redeemer lives and at last he will stand upon the earth" (19:25).

Jesus, the Suffering Messiah, spends his public ministry answering questions about his relationship with God. At his trial the high priest in Jerusalem questions Jesus.

> Jesus answers him, "I have spoken openly to the world; I have always taught in the synagogues and in the temple, I have said nothing secretly. (John 18:20)

Paul's advice to the Colossian saints and servants is an encouraging word:

> Let your speech always be gracious, seasoned with salt, so that you may know how you ought to answer every one. (4:6)

Meditation: Hear my words and those wordless conversations that my soul lifts up to You, O Hearer, O Answerer, of all prayers.

Exodus 19:19   Deuteronomy 27:15   Isaiah 58:9   Matthew 16:16   John 14:23

45 The Embracing One, Saving One  AL-WĀSI'

You shall call his name Jesus, for he will save his people. Matthew 1:21

God the All-Forgiving One has been the subject of two of these names. This name has no biblical linguistic parallels, but there are several references to God who seeks to broaden his care for the world (number 21). Since this name is very close to the common Hebrew word for salvation (*yasha*), there is reasonable inference that the original name in pre-Islamic times was God Al-Yasu', Savior. Both the names of Jesus (*Yesua*) and Joshua are derived from this Hebrew source where the slight changes in the opening y to w sounds and the middle sh to s sounds are consistent with other Hebrew to Arabic words.[1]

A similar linguistic problem is raised by the name for Jesus, which is literally formed with consonants reversed in the Arabic Bible when compared to Jesus' name in the Qur'an. Arab Christians use the pronunciation that is approximate to the biblical name for Jesus (*Yasou'*) while their Muslim neighbors use *'Isa*. The opening and closing sounds are reversed in these two communities of faith. The origins of the Qur'anic name 'Isa are obscure.

Despite these linguistic differences and the far greater ones over the position of Jesus as the divine "Son of God," there are several names which the Qur'an employs to exalt Jesus above other persons. He is distinguished by these titles: Prophet (2:136), strengthened by the Holy Spirit (2:253),[2] Messiah, noble in this world and in the world to come (3:345), confirmed to be the Word (3:340), entrusted with the gospel (57:27).

The thought of God's sending a Redeemer-Savior occurs long before Jesus' physical presence in the Messianic age. The act of the Exodus itself, beginning with the Red Sea crossing, is a redemptive one. "God saved Israel that day from the hand of the Egyptians" (Ex. 14:30). Moses writes prophetically about another prophet who will speak God's word. This prophet will come from among the brethren of Moses (Deut. 18:15).

Another prophet, Isaiah, brings the good tidings that the Saving One will come from the line of David and the gifts of the Spirit will be upon him. These gifts include wisdom, understanding, counsel and might, knowledge and the fear of the Lord (11:2). This prophet, in his description of the Suffering Servant, outlines the path of the Messiah who will be wounded and afflicted, but able to overcome a great humiliation (53:4f). Psalm 22 ends with the promise that the one marked for death will bring "his deliverance to a people yet unborn" (31).

The Gospel of John opens with the pre-existing Word (1:1); it also introduces the Word who "became flesh and dwelled among men" (1:14). The courageous servant of God, John, in his final days writes from exile in the Book of Revelation: "I, John your brother, who share with you in tribulation and the kingdom...in behalf of the Word of God, and the testimony of Jesus" (1:9).

Meditation: My thanks to You, O Embracing and Redeeming Lord, for granting Your Word for my understanding now and forever.

---

1 Samuel 9:16   Psalm 138:7   John 3:17   Acts 7:22   2 Corinthians 6:11   Revelation 19:13

---

[1] Sweetman, vol. 1, p. 19.
[2] Elsewhere, Muslim commentators say that the Spirit is the Archangel Gabriel. See Abdullah Yusuf Ali, *The Holy Qur'an* (New York: Hafner Publishing Company, 1946), sura 17:85, note 2285, p. 719.

46   The Wise

God...give you a spirit of wisdom and of revelation in the knowledge of Jesus Christ. Ephesians 1:17

God the Wise One, Al-Hakim, has already been introduced by God the Judge, number 28, where the same Hebrew and Arabic words reveal several common features in sounds and meanings which persist in both languages today. The Greek word *sophia* appears in numerous English words, including the American word sophomore, a second-year high school or college undergraduate, defined as a "wise fool." This fits the description of a person embodied in the proverb, "A wise son makes a father glad, but a foolish one despises his mother" (Prov. 15:20).

In the Corinthian letters Paul faces the Greek sophisticates head on. He addresses their claims to be wise by calling for a higher wisdom:

> For since, in the wisdom of God, the world did not know God through wisdom, it pleased God through the foolishness of what we proclaim to save those who believe. (1 Cor. 1:21)

Human wisdom is often the opposite of the divine wisdom of the Merciful One, but at the same time, human wisdom, especially from a practical point of view, is highly prized throughout the Bible.

The Wise and Bountiful God empowers skills and information through unnamed wisemen (Ex. 28:3) and wisewomen (Ex. 35:25, 2 Sam. 20:16). Joseph (Gen. 41:35f), David (2 Sam. 14:20), Solomon (2 Chron. 2:12) and Job (chaps. 27,28) exceed all others in wisdom; but each of these praises God for his wise perceptions.

Wise men, prophets and scribes are sent out prior to the coming of Jesus, who later warns the Jerusalemites that these messengers of God face the same threats and death sentences as he was facing (Matt. 23:34). To highlight the servant's inclination to please the master, he asks his followers, "Who then is the faithful and wise servant?" (24:45). He tells a story of wise and foolish bridesmaids who were granted entrance into the marriage feast, based upon whether their lamps were full of oil. This parable is like others that Jesus tells in which subsumed wisdom is required for entrance into the eternal kingdom (25:1f).

The wisdom of this world is not a trustworthy source of revelation, but Paul breaks out in sumptuous praise for the wisdom that God dispenses:

> O the depth of the riches and wisdom and knowledge of God! How unsearchable are his judgments. (Rom. 11:33)

In his closing words to the faithful servants in the Roman capital, Paul presents encouragement:

> For while your obedience is known to all, so that I rejoice over you, I would have you wise as to what is good and guileless as to what is evil. (Rom. 16:19)

Romans' last words offer a benediction: "To the only wise God be glory for evermore through Jesus Christ. Amen" (16:27).

Meditation: O Infinite in knowledge and wisdom, I cry to You for Your gracious understanding that encompasses me like the free air of Your created world.

Deuteronomy 34:9 1 Kings 11:41 Jeremiah 9:23 Daniel 1:4 Colossians 1:28 James 3:13

47 The Beloved, The Affectionate One   اَلْوَدُودُ AL-WADŪD

The God of love and peace will be with you. 2 Corinthians 13:11

God, in this list, is One who shows devotion to his creation. The name Beloved is wrapped within the entire 99 names by overwhelming greatness and generosity. Al-Wadud, which has Hebrew roots, is not the most widely-used word for love in the Bible or the Qur'an. The word *ahab* is a favorite among Arab-speaking Christians, and they use it frequently when they recall "God so loved the world" (John 3:16). The Qur'an restricts its use of this word, ahab, to reveal God's love for "those who do good" (2:195) and not for "those who do wrong" (3:59).

The Persian mystic Jal ad-Din ar-Rumi (d.1273) uses love as the central theme in his voluminous work on Muslim spirituality. He defines love as both desire and need. According to Rumi, God at one time said, "I loved to be known, so I created the world."[1] Rumi also points out that while this attribute of God can be seen in the servants of God, it is only found among humans in a derivative sense, as are all of the other names of God.

God's name is linked to this word in several of the psalms which reveal an affection that lacks the impact of the word steadfast love (*hesed*) that flows throughout the Hebrew scriptures. Al-Wadud's compassionate love is translated as "soul's longing" (Ps. 84:2), "lovely" (84:1), "beloved" (127:2). The last term is found extensively throughout the love affair in the Song of Solomon. The rapturous couple address one another as "my beloved" (2:8) and "my love" (2:10). The word has an endearing quality when used as "uncle" (1 Chron. 27:32).

There are three terms in Greek translated as love which often stray from their strict lexicon meanings when found in the biblical texts. *Eros*, associated with erotic love, was used rarely, as in Galatians 6:14 where Paul states: "My passionate love for the world has been crucified." The highest level of love, *agape*, is spread across scores of pages in the Greek Bible and refers to God's unique love, as in the John 3:16 citation. It encompasses either human love for other humans (Eph. 1:15), or God's name, "God is love" (1 John 4:8), or a general word for love as in the poem of 1 Corinthians 13:1f.

The love for brothers, *philadelphia*, is a term that rests between the two previous words, and fits best this name of God. It is found in 2 Peter 1:17, in a description of the beloved son, and in 1 Peter 3:8:

> "Finally, all of you, have unity of spirit, sympathy, love of the brethren, a tender heart and a humble mind."

The letter to the Hebrew converts states, "Let brotherly love continue" (13:1).

Meditation: My joy from the beginning of my faith in You through Jesus Christ was made complete when I found You as the Beloved Friend.

Deuteronomy 33:12   2 Samuel 7:11f   Isaiah 51:1   Romans 12:10   1 Thessalonians 4:9

---

[1] William C. Chittick, *The Sufi Path of Love* (Albany, NY: SUNY Press, 1983), p. 197.

48   Most Glorious  AL-MAJID

To the Only Wise God, our Savior, through Jesus Christ our Lord, be glory, majesty, dominion and authority, before all time and now and forever. Amen. Jude 25

The themes of the greatness and nobility of the Gracious One permeate this list of the attributes of God. This name appears in the Hebrew Bible with meanings attached to excellency, especially regarding choice fruit and gifts. Moses blesses the people who are about to enter the bountiful land by using the descriptive term *meged* several times in Deuteronomy 33: "choicest gifts" (13), "choicest fruits" (14), and "best gifts of the earth" (16). Song of Solomon also uses this term to describe nature's gifts (4:13).

Both the Hebrew and Greek texts contain sufficient numbers of words translated as glory and glorious. For the Hebrews, glorious means "weighty"; for the Greeks, the word *doxa* is associated with "brightness." The Gospel of Luke (9:30) conveys the glory of the Christ's appearance along with prophets Moses and Elijah. Jesus Christ's inner circle, including Peter, hear the conversation of the three men in the dazzling vision. They speak of Jesus' departure from Jerusalem (9:31). Peter, now the apostle, never forgets this majestic appearance as he discusses in his letter to believers the greater event of the Messiah's resurrection:

> Through [the Suffering Servant] you have confidence in God, who raised him from the dead and gave him glory, so that your faith and hope are in God.
> (1 Peter 1:21)

The apostle exhorts the elder servants of the Messiah not only as witnesses "of the sufferings of Christ, but as future partakers in the glory that is to be revealed" (5:1).

In describing Jesus Christ, from his birth when shepherds saw the angelic glory (Luke 2:9) to his "entering his glory" following his resurrection (Luke 24:26), the New Covenant writers display no restraints in their adoration for Jesus as Lord. Peter, the first evangelist-preacher, connects the fathers and prophets of the past with the present manifestation of God's servant, Jesus:

> The God of Abraham, Isaac and of Jacob, the God of our fathers, glorified his servant, Jesus, whom you delivered up and denied in the presence of Pilate.
> (Acts 3:13)

The first martyr, Stephen, at his death saw in the heavens the glorious God and the Son of Man standing side by side (Acts 7:55f).

The glory of God in the Hebrew Bible is eternal and unchanging. His weighty power is arrayed before the people at the giving of the law to Moses (Ex. 24:16), at the dedication of the temple of Solomon (2 Chron. 7:1), and before Isaiah the prophet while he waits in the temple (Isa. 6:1). However, the glory of the nation, like the fading seasonal flowers (1 Peter 1:24), would come and go. "The glory has departed from Israel" (1 Sam. 4:21) is an oft-repeated refrain through the short Israelite history. The people "exchanged the glory of God for the image of an ox that eats grass" (Ps. 106:20).

Meditation: To You belongs all glory, and nothing can burden or slacken Your great majesty, wisdom and knowledge.

Genesis 45:13   Psalm 63:2   Isaiah 17:4   Ezekiel 43:2   Matthew 4:8   Romans 2:7,10

49 The Resurrector  AL-BĀ'ITH

God has raised up for Israel a Savior, Jesus, as he promised. Acts 13:23

Job asks the question of the resurrection, "If a man dies shall he live again?" (14:14) This is a question that all humanity encounters as part of its lifelong struggle because all know that every form of life must die. This name declares that God is the Resurrector, and also the renewer of life. A more specific word identifying the resurrection of all peoples, and found in both the Bible and the Qur'an, appears later (number 63).

"Never will God raise from the dead anyone who has died," boasted those who rejected the revelations (Sura 16:37). The Qur'an continues to refute these charges by using the first creation as proof that God is able to continue the work of his creation. The one who will resurrect us will be the one who first made us (Sura 17:50). This interpretation of a second creation as part of the resurrection is defended by Al-Ghazali. "The resurrection refers to bringing the dead to life by creating them once more."[1]

It is Paul the apostle who introduces to the Corinthian believers the idea of the "new creation" that is based upon the resurrection of Jesus Christ:

> Therefore, if anyone is in Christ, he is a new creation; the old has passed away,
> lo, the new has come. All of this is from God through Christ. (2 Cor. 5:17,18)

The new creation theme is part of Paul's reasoning with the believers in Galatians who are concerned about keeping the canon, or rule, of the law regarding circumcision (Gal. 6:15,16).

The resurrection involves an accompanying phenomenon, the idea of judgment. Daniel's view of a resurrection is straightforward and quite developed for his time, hundreds of years before Jesus Christ:

> Many who sleep in the dust of the earth shall awake; some to everlasting life,
> and some to shame and everlasting contempt. (Dan. 12:2)

The relationship with his heavenly Father was so strong that it allowed Jesus to say openly that he had authority to execute judgment when the dead will hear and "come forth, those who have done good, to the resurrection of life, and those who have done evil, to the resurrection of judgment" (John 5:29).

Jesus' disclosures of the Son of Man included this teaching: "For judgment I came into this world" (John 9:39). He concludes a parable with the remark that a generous host will be "repaid at the resurrection of the just" (Luke 14:14).

Meditation: My existence on this planet is so tentative; I have no God but You who give me the hope of a resurrection, O generous Creator.

Matthew 27:53   Hebrews 6:2   Ephesians 5:14   1 Corinthians 15:12,13,21,42

---

[1] Al-Ghazali, p. 123.

50 The Witness  ASH-SHAHĪD

Jesus Christ, the faithful witness, the first-born of the dead, and the ruler of kings on earth. Revelation 1:5

This name for God has two significant meanings in both Greek and Arabic. Ash-Shahid can mean witness and martyr. In the Greek Bible *martus* means either witness or martyr. Neither of these words appears in the Hebrew portions of scripture. But for both God and man, the main idea of witness is one who tells the truth; and that is consistent throughout the whole Bible.

The earliest church history is contained in short summaries in the Book of Acts. This book of the Christian canon could also be named the Acts of the Holy Spirit or the Acts of the Witnesses of the Resurrection of Jesus. Jesus speaks to his followers shortly before his rising to heaven:

> But you shall receive power when the Holy Spirit has come upon you; and shall be my witnesses in Jerusalem and in all Judea and Samaria and to the end of the earth. (1:8)

From these earliest days, the apostles and their growing convert community continue "their witness to the resurrection of the Lord Jesus; and great grace was upon them all" (4:33). Stephen completes his oral witness and his martyrdom when he is cast out of the city and stoned to death for blasphemy. Present at his death are the legal witnesses who cast stones at him. Saul, the prosecuting zealot, is among those witnesses who consented to Stephen's death (7:58f).

Saul becomes Paul after his own conversion experience on the road to Damascus (9:1f); he begins a new life, refuting his past opposition to the people of The Way, the designated name of the early church (9:2). In his own court hearings, Paul bears witness not only to his former life as an enemy of The Way, but to his new calling, a witness to the Gentiles (22:4,20,21). Paul ends his days like Stephen, both a witness and a martyr in Rome, where he calls upon both great and small in proclaiming the "kingdom of God, and teaching about the Lord Jesus Christ" (28:30).

Any Bible reader will find that the act of witnessing is a well-conceived and well-executed part of the legal-justice system. The ninth commandment expressly forbids giving false witness (Ex. 20:16). A single witness is not sufficient in a capital case, and there are other restrictions on witnesses in minor cases (Deut. 19:15f). An elaborate guide for witnessing the purchase of property is detailed in the Book of Ruth (4:9f).

The taking of oaths is a common practice during the whole biblical period. God is often called as the third party witness: with Jacob (Gen. 31:50), Joshua (24:27), Samuel (1 Sam. 12:5). Paul in his most important letter takes a similar oath:

> God is my witness, whom I serve with my spirit in the gospel of his Son, that without ceasing I mention you in my prayers. (Rom. 1:9)

Meditation: Your life given for me, spared my life; for this I will give witness.

Proverbs 24:28   Isaiah 43:10   Jeremiah 42:5   John 1:9   Luke 24:48   Revelation 20:4

51 The Truth  AL-HAQQ

Jesus said, "I am the way, and the truth, and the life." John 14:6

This word is closely aligned to Jesus' own life's witness that opened with the Gospel of John proclaiming him, "The Word became flesh and dwelt among us, full of grace and truth" (1:14). His public ministry closes when he faces the Roman governor and chooses not to answer Pilate's question, "What is truth?" (18:38). In between these two episodes, Jesus declares himself the way, the truth, and the life. These three words find close affinities within the 99 names, beginning with the Truth. Jesus's identification with the Way has been established by Acts 9:2 and is comparable to name number 94, the Guider, while Life is approximate to name number 62, the Ever-living, the Alive.

The Hebrew word has the same word structure as Haqq, which also has some differences in its meaning, translated decrees and statutes. The Arabic term is translated as truth and right. Often these meanings overlap, especially when referring to God's decrees, as in the ordinance for the first Passover meal in Egypt (Ex. 12:24), a festival decree (Ps. 81:5,6), statutes (Ps. 119:5). The word *huqqah* occurs twenty times in Psalm 119.

When a Hebrew writer wants to express truth, as opposed to falsehood, the words selected come from the roots of the words "belief" and "Amen" (name 6). God is "a God of truth" (Deut. 32:4, Isa. 65:16 and Zech. 8:8). Peace and truth are combined in a number of passages found in Isaiah (39:8), Jeremiah (33:6) and Esther (9:30). In both the Hebrew and Greek, God's blessings fall upon those who are messengers of the truth of God. The good servant-king Hezekiah did what was true before the Lord, and whatever work he proposed to do prospered (2 Chron. 31:21).

David's trust in the Lord is a thorough confidence, as attested by several of the psalms attributed to him:

> Into your hand I commit my spirit; you have redeemed me, O Lord, true God.
> (Ps. 31:5)

A later psalm praises both God and David for not wavering in trust. "The Lord swears to David a sure truth from which he will not turn back" (Ps. 132:11).

The Greek Bible writers are concerned with conveying absolute truth, as John points out to his readers. "God is spirit and those who worship him must worship him in spirit and truth" (4:24). Jesus' words continues, "You shall know the truth and the truth will make you free" (8:32), and finally, to his disciples he offers this hope about the one sent to act in his stead:

> I will pray the Father, and he will give you another Counselor, to be with you forever, the Spirit of Truth. (John 14:17)

When Pontius Pilate washes his hands of Jesus and thus opens up the way for the crucifixion, the unanswered question "What is truth?" is still on this Roman official's mind (18:38). Pilate knows already the facts of Jesus' life, but he does not have those intimate details that are available to Jesus' small band of followers. Pilate asks the right question, but lacks the spiritual understanding to take a step toward finding the true answer.

Meditation: O my True One, my tongue and my actions cannot dispel Your matchless life of unmixed purity. O my God, forgive me.

Isaiah 30:8   Jeremiah 32:11   Zechariah 7:8   Matthew 22:16   Romans 2:2   1 John 1:6,8

52   The Enabler, The Trustee    AL-WAKĪL

I can do all things through Christ who gives me strength. Philippians 4:13

In biblical times face-to-face meetings other than social affairs were avoided and handed over to a powerful *wakil*, steward, who served his master in both good and evil days. This epithet for God comes from the Hebrew and Aramaic roots meaning to be able, have power, and is used as a common verb or auxiliary verb in the Bible. In the Greek, the steward's position is subordinate to his master, but the emphasis in the parables of Jesus and in the Epistles is on empowerment and faithful relationships. Contemporary Arabic words abound that refer to business, legal, military and government agencies that use this word as their source.

One time when Jesus is teaching a large crowd, a father of an epileptic boy interrupts the gathering. He apologizes to Jesus by saying that he has asked Jesus' closest disciples to heal his son. Jesus rebuked the demon that caused the boy's illness and went on to also rebuke his disciples for their inability to heal the epileptic. He tells them in private that they can not heal the boy because of their lack of faith. He concludes that, "faith as a grain of mustard seed" will enable them to remove mountains and "nothing will be impossible to you" (Matt. 17:14-20).

On another day, Jesus is addressed by a rich young ruler: "Good Teacher, what shall I do to inherit eternal life?" (Luke 18:18). After inquiring about his faithfulness in keeping the law, Jesus says, "One thing you still lack. Sell all that you have and distribute to the poor" (22). Luke reports that the man was very sad. "But Jesus looking at him says, 'It is easier for a camel to go through an eye of a needle than for a rich man to enter the kingdom of God'" (25). He speaks again the words to Peter, who questions him about family commitments, "What is impossible with men is possible with God" (27).

In both these episodes, Jesus presents his followers with a situation that appeared impossible for them to resolve by human standards—removing a mountain by speaking to it, and ordering a camel to go through the eye of a needle. Jesus, the master teacher, uses these impossible demands to show that he is ready to help, to empower, to take on impossible tasks in advancing the kingdom. Later, when these former helpless disciples are courageously expanding their faith, they call upon the Empowering One to accomplish difficult works of faith—not the meaningless task of removing a mountain, but bringing men and women into the kingdom of God.

Peter stands before the Jerusalem crowds some fifty days after the resurrection and claims that he is a witness of Jesus Christ through the power of the Holy Spirit (Acts 5:32f). He writes later as a church leader to his fellow servants to be "good stewards of God's varied grace" (1 Peter 4:10).

Meditation: In my happiest moments when I sense Your presence, O loving God, I know that You are my owner and I can trust You.

Genesis 15:2   2 Chronicles 28:1   Luke 16:2-4   Titus 1:7   1 Corinthians 4:1,2

53 The Powerful ٱلْقَوِيُّ AL-QAWI

To both Jews and Greeks, Christ the Power of God. 1 Corinthians 1:24

This name returns us to a familiar theme within the 99 names that speaks of the greatness, strength, and might of God. A natural, human division exists between the merciful and gentle names and the more severe names, like this one for the All-Powerful One. But in the great mystery of God's unity there is only one essence, and all of these manifestations within the names of God are human images of this unity. The followers of Jesus Christ see him as part of this unity, since the Scriptures faithfully represent his receiving power from his heavenly Father.

There are two Greek words that denote power in the Gospels, Letters and the Book of Acts. They are both found in Acts 1:7, 8 where Jesus answers his disciples' questions about the return of the kingdom to Israel:

> It is not for you to know the times or seasons which the Father has fixed for his own authority (*exousia*). But you will receive power (*dunamis*), when the Holy Spirit comes upon you and you shall be my witnesses to...the ends of the earth.

In this reading of Acts, these two Greek words differentiate between original authority (exousia) and delegated power (dunamis). However, in the Gospels, Jesus has both original powers and powers that are given to him directly from God. He holds power to forgive sins, and indicates in his disputations with the Jews (Matt. 9:6, 8) that this was from God. He also delegates to his disciples the authority to cast out evil spirits (10:1) and, at the close of ministry, he claims, "All authority in heaven and on earth has been given to me" (Matt. 28:18).

The letters covering the spread of the faith continued to blur the differences between the two words. For example, in Acts 1:7, 8, Paul writes that "every soul [should] be subject to governing authorities," adding in the same breath, "there is no authority but from God" (Rom. 13:1). In the second Corinthian letter, Paul reminds his readers that "the transcendent power belongs to God and not to us" (4:7); yet the servants of God are endowed with "the Holy Spirit, genuine love, truthful speech, and the power of God" (6:6, 7). Many images emerge from the Book of Revelation, but none is quite as inscrutable as the myriad voices shouting, "Worthy is the Lamb who was slain, to receive power and wealth and wisdom and might and honor and glory" (Rev. 5:12).

All the literary clues within this vision in Revelation come from the Hebrew Bible, including the reference to wealth, heavy, *kabod*, which forms part of God's power and strength. The Hebrew word for power is a twin to the Arabic word, in pronunciation and meaning. The subject of power is varied. It refers to God in creation in Jeremiah 10:12 and God governing the world in Psalm 65:7. Other biblical characters lost power as did Samson (Judg. 16:5f) and David, who lost the power to weep (1 Sam. 30:4).

Meditation: God, You are the source of all power and might. May my attention be drawn to You as the source of humbleness and truth.

Genesis 49:3   Isaiah 49:4   Hosea 13:14   Luke 1:35   Romans 8:38   2 Peter 1:3,6

54 The Firm One  AL-MATĪN

*Of old thou didst lay the foundation of the earth, and the
heavens are the work of thy hands.* Psalms 102:25

A number of references in the Hebrew Bible apply to the foundations of the Temple in Jerusalem. The first temple of Solomon is celebrated in 2 Chronicles 23:5; the second temple in Ezra 3:11. When both of these were destroyed, as was a third one in 70 A.D., the people of God saw there was something greater than man-made temples. The writer of Hebrews often alludes to a greater house in which Christ was greater than a steward:

> But Christ was faithful over God's house as a son. And we are his house if we hold fast our confidence and pride in our hope. (3:6)

Jesus faces a simple problem on every turn as he preaches the gospel of the kingdom. There are those who hear and respond immediately by saying, "Lord, Lord" and yet do not do what Jesus tells them (Luke 6:46). On one occasion these listeners are compared to seeds that fall on shallow ground, and because they have no roots, they spring forth and die soon after (Matt.13:5,21). In the Gospel of Luke, Jesus tells the story about two men who built houses on two different foundations. The point of the story comes at the end with Jesus' practical observation about listening:

> But he who hears and does not do them [my words] is like a man who built a house on the ground without a foundation...when the stream broke, it fell, and the ruin of that house was great. (Luke 6:49)

The subject of a good, firm foundation is on Paul's mind when he writes the first letter to the Corinthians. In chapter 3, he mentions foundation-laying three times. He calls himself a master builder who lays a foundation that others should build carefully upon (10). Jesus Christ is the foundation—there is no other (11) and the foundation's building materials, from hay to gold and silver (12), will be tried by fire to "test what sort of work each man has done" and will be rewarded accordingly (13-15).

God's faithful servants bear testimony of a special bonding which is sealed by an oath in the name of the Lord.

> God's firm foundation stands, bearing this seal: "The Lord knows those who are his," and, "Let everyone who names the name of the Lord depart from iniquity." (2 Tim. 2:29)

Meditation: I need no other argument, I need no other plea; it is enough that Jesus died, and that He died for me.[1]

Numbers 20:8   2 Kings 11:2   Psalm 45:6   Amos 3:12   Hebrews 11:10   Revelation 21:14

---

[1] Lidie Edmunds, "My Faith Has Found a Resting Place," in *Hymns* (Chicago: Inter-Varsity Press, 1952), no. 97.

55 The Protecting Friend — أَلْوَلِيُّ AL-WALĪ

No longer do I call you servants...but I have called you friends. John 15:15

Islam developed its own mysticism shortly after the death of Muhammad in 632 A.D. Once a man or a woman entered into a religious community, he or she took on the name of a friend of God, *wali Allah*, after the Qur'anic verse, "Lo, the friends of God, there is no fear upon them, neither do they grieve" (10:36). A mystic, or Sufi, who rises to the highest level of spiritual enlightenment is called wali, a title much like saint in the Western church. The Bible languages do not have any words that are equivalent to this name for God. However, the idea of friend, saint, and guardian are close to the Scriptures.

When Jesus meets with his inner circle of followers in the dark night of his betrayal and arrest, he has much on his mind to share with them. John, the beloved disciple, is able to later write some of Jesus' conversation with his disciples. He recalls the words that the Messiah spoke, even while the disciple Judas Iscariot was making a deal to betray Jesus for thirty pieces of silver (Matt. 26:14).

Jesus opens his heart even further to those who were still with him. He speaks about love for one another; and John, the gospel writer, uses the highest level of love in the Greek language to describe what Jesus said to these disciples:

> This is the commandment, that you love one another as I have loved you. Greater love has no man than this, that a man lay down his life for his friends. (John 15:12,13)

When John the apostle reports on Jesus' word for friends, he selects the second level word for love, *fileo*, to designate the degree of friendship.

The highest compliments that are paid to the prophets Abraham and Moses come when they are called friends of God. In 2 Chronicles 20:7 and James 2:23, Abraham is not remembered for any of the details of his great life of faith, except that he is "called the friend of God." The life of Moses is summarized in this reference from Exodus: "Thus the Lord used to speak to Moses face to face, as a man spoke to his friend" (33:11).

"A friend loves at all times, and a brother is born to adversity," says the proverb (Prov. 17:17), indicating that friendship is based upon a selection process not connected to blood or clan lines. Jesus' choices may have started in a servant-master relationship, but he elevates his close disciples to be with him, not as inferiors but as uniquely non-blood brothers, a family.

The Bible warns regarding insincere and deceptive friendships, as in the case of Judas, one of the twelve, who betrays his master with a kiss (Mark 14:44). Job complains, "All of my intimate friends abhor me" (19:19). "Have no confidence in a friend" expresses the sentiments of the prophet Micah (7:5). Paul closes his first Corinthian letter in his own hand, "If any one has no love (fileo) for the Lord, let him be accursed" (16:22).

Meditation: May my inner love and my friendships be part of Your plan for me to reach out to those who are friendless in this world.

Isaiah 41:8   Psalm 38:11   Proverbs 19:4   John 11:11   Mark 5:19   James 4:4

56   The Praiseworthy ٱلْحَمِيدُ AL-ḤAMĪD

Praise our God, all you his servants, you who fear him, small and great.
Revelation 19:5

The names Muhammad, Ahmed, Hamid are well recognized derivatives of this name for God, which is very close to a Hebrew word with the same linguistic make-up. When the word appears in the Hebrew, it is often close to this admonition as found in the commandment "You shall not covet" (Ex. 20:17).

In several other biblical references evil desires and secular delights are condemned and, when the nation and people seek pleasure in idolatry (Isa. 1:29), lusting for a woman (Prov. 6:25), lusting for young men (Ezek. 23:6), and pleasant vineyards (Amos 5:11). However, the rarer Hebrew-Aramaic sources point to praise. In Psalm 68:18, the Lord is praised in a highly poetic verse:

> Thou didst ascend the high mountain, leading captives in thy train, and received praise among men.

The favorite Hebrew word for praise is found in the expression "Hallelujah" (praise to *Yahweh*), which permeates the entire Bible and is universally recognized. The last chapters in the Psalms are filled with the praise hymns that were part of the temple worship. The hallelujahs abound, like this one:

> Praise the Lord! For it is good to sing praises to our God; he is gracious, and a song of praise is seemly. (Ps. 147:1)

The following psalm (148) involves not only the voices of the Levitical choirs and worshipers but the sounds of supernaturals and nature crying out in joyful praises:

> Hallelujah! Praise the Lord from the heavens, praise him in the heights! Praise him, all his angels, praise him all his hosts. Praise him, sun and moon, praise him shining stars! Let them praise the name of the Lord! For he commanded and they were created. (148:1-5).

As Jesus rides the donkey into the gates of the city, he gladly accepts the voices of praise and rebukes his enemies by quoting Psalm 8:2, "Out of the mouths of babes and sucklings thou hast perfect praise" (Matt. 21:16). Luke adds the details that Jesus will not tell those who were praising him to restrain their voices because: "If these were silent the very stones would cry out" (19:39,40). Three gospel writers report that the crowds shouted the word-phrase, "Hosanna" (Save, we pray thee).

> Hosanna! Blessed is he who comes in the name of the Lord! Blessed is the kingdom of our father David that is coming. (Mark 11:9,10 and John 12:13)

The writer of Hebrews encourages Jesus' followers to offer praises much as the high priest offers a sacrifice in the temple:

> Let us continually offer up a sacrifice of praise to God; that is, the fruit of our lips to acknowledge [Jesus'] name. (13:15)

Meditation: The whole creation praises You, O my Maker; my soul responds in great praises for Your gifts of salvation and life.

---

1 Chronicles 29:13   Psalms 48:10, 113:1   Isaiah 53:2   Luke 2:13,20   1 Peter 1:7

57 The Reconciler   أَلْمُحْصِي AL-MUHSI

If he has wronged you at all...charge that to my account. Philemon 18

The Greek and the Arabic origins of their respective early abacuses provide the background for this one of the 99 names of God. God the Reckoner, Al-Hasib, has been previously viewed as number 40 in this list and shares qualities with Al-Muhsi. The Hebrew does not have a Bible word that means "little stones," "pebbles" and "calculate" as do the Greek and Arabic with their root words to this attribute of the All-Wise God.

The apostle Paul writes a personal letter in his own hand to Philemon, the owner of a runaway slave, Onesimus. Paul, himself confined as a Roman prisoner, makes a direct appeal for Philemon to accept Onesimus, who is the bearer of the letter. Paul asserts in the short appeal that Onesimus is no longer a slave but a "beloved brother," and the apostle promises to make good any further debts that the former slave has left behind. "Charge this to my account" (v. 18) would become a metaphor for the new faith in Jesus Christ.

Jesus uses a couple of short parabolic statements that may be part of the local news at the time when he is speaking. He introduces the subject of the cost of discipleship by telling his close followers that any builder should first sit down and "count the cost" of the entire project or face embarrassment at only a foundation and an unfinished tower (Luke 14:29). The second analogy concerns a king who who with his trusted counselors has to make a decision about facing an army twice as strong as the king's. The king makes overtures for peace while the enemy is "yet a great way off" (14:32).

According to any human accounting system, a righteous Pharisee is superior to the tax collector who stands beside him. The tax collector is overcome by the merits of the Pharisee who fasts weekly and pays tithes to the temple. The tax collector looks downward in despair, saying, "God, be merciful to me a sinner!" (Luke 18:9-14). The reply of Jesus provides a clear illustration of human redemption by a God who is an Accountant/Reconciler of incredible mercy. Jesus says that the tax collector:

> Went down to his house justified rather than the other; for every one who exalts himself will be humbled. (v. 14)

In the Greek Bible reconciliation is a key word that has its origin in God's unique "reckoning" with Abraham in Genesis 15:6: Abraham "believed the Lord; and he reckoned it to him as righteousness." Jesus' radical teaching about God's justification in contrast to human self-justification is part of the New Covenant message that Paul teaches the early believers: "through Jesus Christ," the world is being reconciled to God by "making peace by the blood of the cross" (Col. 1:20).

Meditation: O Eternal Lord, I praise You for Your generous, reconciling love that lifts me up to You; and for that I cannot boast.

Genesis 31:15   Psalm 44:22   1 Chronicles 7:5,7   Romans 5:10   2 Corinthians 5:17

58   The Originator, The Innovator   ٱلْمُبْدِئ AL-MUBDĪ

For it was fitting that he, Jesus Christ,...should become the pioneer of their salvation through suffering. Hebrews 2:10

Al-Mubdi, the Beginner at creation, can be added to the three names, numbers 11, Creator, 12, the Maker, the Creator, and 13, the Fashioner, which regard God as the Originator of all life. This Arabic word is close to a rare Hebrew word with the same vocalizations, but which refers to human innovation and invention. In the declining years of the Israelite monarchy, one of the kings devises a holiday for one of the foreign gods (1 Kings 12:33), and an enemy of the Jews invented a false charge against the people of God at the building of the second temple (Neh. 6:8).

Remarkably, to be called an innovator within certain circles of thought today is considered a grave infraction of religious and moral canons. For an earlier example, the use of prayer beads, the *subha*, to recite the 99 names of God was despised as an innovation when it was introduced three centuries after the first years of Islam. Another event that is still considered *bid'a* in a rigidly conservative nation, like Saudi Arabia, is the celebration of the prophet's birthday and adding grave markers in cemeteries.[1]

The idea of innovation in a good sense first belongs to God as the only One who does create from nothing. On the other hand, God's people accept both God's new things and human invention as positive forces in building a society. "Newness" is a favorite word for the prophet Isaiah who uses it throughout his prophecies. The Lord will make a "new sharp threshing floor" (41:15) and a "new name for the city of Jerusalem" (62:2), and the eschatological promise is "a new heaven and a new earth" (66:22).

"In the beginning" opens both the Book of Genesis and the Gospel of John. For readers of the Arabic Bible, the term beginning is closely tied to Al-Kalam, the Word, who was in the beginning with God (John 1:1,2). The Qur'an recognizes that the title, God's Word, along with Messiah, son of Mary of the Spirit, belongs to Jesus (4:171). While the Qur'an denies any divinity to Christ, it does say that "the Messiah does not disdain to be a servant of God" (172).[2]

When Jesus prepares the Passover meal in what is his last meal with his disciples, he changes the old Jewish custom by his personal involvement in the bread and wine:

> This is my blood of the New Covenant, which is poured out for many. Truly, I say to you, I shall not drink again of the fruit of the vine until that day when I drink it new in the kingdom of God. (Mark 14:24,25)

Jesus is introduced as the "mediator of the New Covenant" according to Hebrews 12:24.

Meditation: Begin and begin again Your new creation in me.

Judges 5:8   Jeremiah 31:31   Mark 1:27   1 Corinthians 11:25   Colossians 3:10

---

[1] Ignaz Goldziher, *Introduction to Islamic Theology and Law* (Princeton: University Press, 1981), p. 233.

[2] The Koran, p. 78.

59 The Restorer ﺍﻟْﻤُﻌِﻴْﻦ AL-MU'ID

Jesus said to him, "Stretch out your hand." And he did so, and his hand was restored.
Luke 6:10

Even in the Hebrew Bible where this word has an affinity to the Arabic, Al-Mu'id, the connections with healing and physical restoration are undeniable. The basic idea of Al-Mu'id is one who will return but also will be the restorer in all areas of human life. In Psalm 23, an exhausted sheep can depend upon the Shepherd who "restores the soul" (2). Another psalm opens with hallelujahs to praise God for "opening the eyes of the blind" and lifting up "those who are bowed down" (146:8) and continues with, "The Lord watches over the sojourners, he restores the widow and the fatherless" (9).

The restorative ministry of Jesus Christ is announced in good tidings from the prophet Isaiah, over seven centuries before Jesus' birth to Mary:

> The Spirit of the Lord God is upon me because the Lord has anointed me to bring good news to the afflicted; he has sent me to bind up the brokenhearted, to proclaim liberty to the captives, and the opening of the prison to those who are bound; to proclaim the year of the Lord's favor. (Isa. 61:1,2)

Jesus uses this text to preach to his countrymen in the Nazareth synagogue in a Sabbath day service. Sitting down at the close of the above Isaiah readings, he declares: "Today this scripture has been fulfilled in your hearing" (Luke 4:21). Luke reports Jesus' hometown attackers and also the fact of Jesus' citing two cases from the Hebrew Bible recording miraculous restoration-healings. Both involve outsiders to the Jewish establishment. The widow whose son is raised from the dead lives in the border area of Lebanon where the prophet Elijah performed the miracle (1 Kings 17:8f). The second healing mentioned by Jesus involves Elijah's successor, the prophet Elisha, who heals the Syrian commander, Naaman, of leprosy (2 Kings 5:1).

Elijah, the great prophet of Israel, is on the minds of many of Jesus' contemporaries. One day Jesus answers the question about Elijah's returning and "restoring all things" prior to the coming of the Messiah. He says, "Elijah has already come and they do not know him." He also says that he will suffer as the Son of Man, and the disciples recognized the association of John the Baptist with the Hebrew prophet (Matt. 17:11f).

In the Book of James, Elijah is honored for his faithful prayers to God for first withholding rain for over three years and then for rain that restores the land (5:17). Elijah is cited as a "man of like nature with ourselves," as he shows that after his mighty deeds he needs the assurances of God's care to restore his spiritual well-being. The servant of God who is spiritually capable "should restore" a brother overcome with sin "in the spirit of gentleness" (Gal. 6:1).

Meditation: The present world offers little favors for what it extracts from my life. But You, O Sustainer of my soul, promise to restore all that is good and nourishing to eternal life.

Genesis 20:7,14 Psalm 147:6 Daniel 9:25 Mark 3:5 Acts 1:6 James 5:5

60   The Giver of Life   ٱلْمُحْيِي AL-MUḤYĪ

Whoever lives and believes in me shall never die. John 11:26

On the day that the parents of John the Baptist dedicate their infant son, there is a heated debate over the name that God has given to both parents (Luke 1:13,59f). John in Arabic is *Yahiya*, God lives, and that name identifies both Muslim and Christian Arabs, but the Arabic Bible refers to another name, *Yohanah* (God is gracious), for John the Baptist. The Hebrew *chai* is a mirror image of the Arabic *hayy*, which is the root of this name for God as it appears in number 62 of these beautiful names.

The Genesis account of creation proclaims that God created all living creatures (1:21) and that all life was to be renewed "according to their kinds" (1:24); Adam became a living being by the breath of God (2:7) while Eve would be known as the "mother of all living" (Gen. 3:20). The creation story and life itself are wrapped in mysteries, yet the living God is pleased to share his creative powers with all other living things. Men and women, as well as all other living organisms, enjoy this life force which is derived from God.

The living and life-giving God is hailed by Joshua for delivering the people safely to the land of promise (3:10), by David at his victory over his enemies (2 Sam. 22:47), and by King Hezekiah in a prayer of national repentance. The king's cry is included in Isaiah's prophecy when he speaks for another and for himself after the Lord has restored his health: "The living, the living, he thanks thee, as I do this day" (Isa. 38:19). Isaiah's vision of the Suffering Servant is of one who is "cut off from the land of the living" and who "made his grave with the rich man in his death" (Isa. 53:8,9).

The report of Jesus' healings of a blind person and a leper is found in a Qur'anic sentence where he also restores the dead to life (5:109/110). This same Sura 5, in a discussion of Cain and Abel, is quoted for the Israelite tradition which states that "whoever kills a human being...shall be looked upon as though he had killed all mankind." The reverse also is true. "Whoever saves a life shall be regarded as though he had saved all mankind" (5:32).[1]

The meticulous explanations of the death and resurrection of Jesus Christ in all four Gospels have a prototype in the Gospel of John's story of the raising of Lazarus. When Jesus arrives with his followers in Bethany, Lazarus has been dead four days (11:17). At the same time sizable numbers of people either are attracted to his message or, like the Jewish religious leaders, are seeking to cut him off from his followers (11:8). At the graveside, Jesus speaks to his Heavenly Father where he shows concern for the people nearby, "that they might believe that you did send me" (John 11:42).

Lazarus comes out of the grave at Jesus' command. He is unbound and let go. But the divisions within the populace grow deeper—some believe while others join with the groups opposing him in their unbelief (John 11:45f).

Meditation: All thanks to You, O Living and Creating One.

Genesis 45:5   Job 33:30   Psalm 16:11   John 4:10,11   1 Peter 3:7,10   Revelation 7:17

---

[1] *The Koran*, p. 83.

61   Giver of Death

The Lord kills and brings to life; he brings down to Sheol and raises up. 1 Samuel 2:6

The preceding four names, Al-Muhsi, Al-Mubdi, Al-Mu'id, and Al-Muhyi, form a rhyming pattern of the "mu" syllable. This present name, Al-Mumit, creator of death, continues this rhyme scheme but this time the "mu" is part of the word itself and not a prefix, as is the case in the other names (57-60). With Al-Mumit, there is a return to the severe names for God which quality is apparent in some of the earlier names (20-25) when the severe names were paired with the merciful names: The Honorer/Dishonorer. With this name there is a merciful name on each side, which numbers 60 and 62, speaks of "Life" as opposed to death. This triple effect will appear again in this list.

The Hebrew is consistent with the Arabic in this name so that the modern Hebrew and modern Arabic Bibles pronounce the word "death" similarly.

When Jesus first hears about Lazarus, he does not make any haste to be with his sick friend nor to comfort the two distressed sisters. He sends word to them, "This sickness is not unto death; but is for the glory of God" (Luke 11:4). These consoling words are not enough for Mary and Martha to overcome their fear of death; this fear is described in the Letter to the Hebrews as a condition for all humanity as a "lifelong bondage" (2:15). This great fear of the inevitable is an underlying cause of much of our conscious, but more likely of our unconscious, human behavior.

Death's power is evident throughout the Hebrew scriptures, as even deceased bodies had to be carefully attended to (Lev. 21:11). The prophet warns against "consulting the dead in behalf of the living" (Isa. 8:19), and the fear of the unknown, shadowy regions of Sheol awaits all who die. King David's triumphal song at the victory over his rival includes this sorrowful note: "The cords of Sheol entangled me, the snares of death confronted me" (2 Sam. 22:6). A later psalm was more hopeful:

> For you did not give me up to Sheol, or let your godly one see the Pit. You showed me the path of life. (Ps. 16:10,11)

Jonah prays from "the belly of Sheol," and the answer comes, for he also prays, "Yet you did bring up my life from the Pit" (Jonah 2:2,6).

Later prophets are more discriminating about the habitations of those who die. The polytheists will be thrust in death down to the Pit and a worthy person will enjoy an Edenic paradise, according to Ezekiel 28:8f. The prophet Daniel states that those who are asleep in death's dust will awake to either "everlasting life" or "shame and everlasting contempt" (Dan. 12:2).

The Lord speaks to his servants through Peter about divine forbearance; God is "not wishing that any should die, but that all should reach repentance," thus saving some from the coming fiery destruction of the earth (2 Peter 3:9f).

Meditation: Your words and Your promises to me, my Savior-Word, are my guides to the path leading through death's anguish.

Genesis 23:3   Ecclesiastes 4:2   Psalm 34:22   Amos 2:2   Matthew 8:22   Acts 3:15

62   The Ever-Living, The Alive   أَلْحَىُّ AL-HAYY

The life was made manifest, and we saw it, and testify to it,
and proclaim to you the eternal life. 1 John 1:2

Al-Hayy is the second in Jesus' names for himself based upon John 14:6. The trilogy consists of Way, Truth and Life and will be summed up with the "I Am's" of Jesus in name number 94. The widely-recognized Muslim mystic Jal ad-Din dr-Rumi acknowledges Jesus' power over death: "Jesus' breath may bring you to life and make it like itself: beautiful and auspicious."[1] The Mighty Lord selects the name *Yahweh*, meaning living (*chayah*), to reintroduce himself to Moses (Ex. 3:13f). This forms a confession found on the lips of Jesus:

> "...the God of Abraham, and the God of Isaac, and the God of Jacob. He is not the God of the dead, but the living." (Matt. 22:32)

In Deuteronomy, at the delivery of the Commandments, Moses hears the voice of God and witnesses to the "living God speaking out of the midst of fire" (5:26). The prophet Jeremiah adds "living" to God's attributes of truth and royal power: "But the Lord is the true God; he is the living God and the everlasting King" (10:10). Psalm 121:4 exalts the Lord who "will neither slumber nor sleep," which the Qur'an cites in the following:

> Put your trust in the Ever-living (Al-Hayy) who never dies. Celebrate his praise. He knows well all his servant's sins. He created the heavens and earth in six days. (Sura 25:58)

The subject of life and mortality is an essential part of Jesus' spoken ministry to both his friends and his detractors. He discloses himself as the Son who is closest to the heavenly, eternal One, the Father. Jesus states with confidence, "For as the Father has life in himself, so he has granted the Son also to have life in himself" (John 5:26). After the death and resurrection of Jesus Christ, John sums up his purposes for writing:

> These things are written that you may believe that Jesus is the Christ, the Son of God, and that believing you may have life in his name. (John 20:31)

Later the apostle John, writes to his fellow servants: "By this we know love, that he laid down his life for us; and we ought to lay down our lives for the brethren" (1 John 3:16).

The Gospels end where the Book of the Acts, the Epistles and the Revelation begin—at the death and resurrection of Jesus Christ. This event is remembered by Paul as the most important good tidings in his life.

> That Christ died for our sins in accordance with the scripture, that he was buried, that he was raised on the third day in accordance with the scriptures. (1 Cor. 15:3,4)

Later in this same chapter, Paul quotes from Hosea who hails the triumph of life over death, "Death is swallowed up in victory. O death where is thy sting?" (15:54, Hos. 13:14). This victory forms the basis of the faith of all who name the name of God in Christ.

Meditation: All praise to You, my sovereign Lord, for raising the dead and giving me a lively hope in the coming life.

Genesis 12:13   Deuteronomy 30:15,19   Proverbs 21:21   John 1:4   Revelation 12:11

---

[1] Chittick, p. 282.

63 Self-Subsisting, The Resurrected One — AL-QAYYUM

Jesus said, "I am the resurrection and the life; he who believes in me, though he die, yet shall he live. John 11:25

The Hebrew and the Arabic root to this name are similar, and extend to a number of related terms in both languages. While the original idea for the word is to stand upright, erect, arise, the word takes on a significant religious meaning when it is used to describe the raising of the dead. The Qur'an, the Greek Bible and the Arabic Bible use this term and its variants to express "resurrection."

Another Qur'anic word for the Resurrector, Al-Ba'ith, number 49, is the favored word for raising the dead in the Qur'an. Other terms related to Ar-Rafi' (number 23) are used to announce the "raising up of Jesus" (Sura 4:157f). When it speaks about the resurrection day, the Qur'an prefers the term *youm al-qiyama* (3:55, 5:14 and 75:1,6).

Once the children of Israel pass through the waters at Jericho, Joshua orders them to erect an altar of twelve stones to celebrate the entry into Canaan (Josh. 4:9). Another use of the word has a practical application for Ruth the Moabitess when she formalizes her marriage to the Bethlehem native, Boaz. At that time she plans to raise up, or restore, the name of her former, now deceased husband. This contract establishes the fact that she is redeemed by her kinsman and that the dead will not be cut off from any further inheritance (Ruth 4:4f).

There is a special use of the phrase "lifting up one's eyes" that is found in the story that Jesus told about the rich man and the poor man Lazarus when both died and went to their separate destinies of hell/sheol and heaven (Luke 16:19f). Lazarus, not the same person who was raised from the dead earlier (John 11), goes to "Abraham's bosom." The rich man raises up his eyes and implores Father Abraham to send Lazarus to wet his lips in the midst of the flames of torment. The request is denied, and Jesus adds this comment designed for his unresponsive listeners:

> If they do not hear Moses and the prophets, neither will they be convinced if someone should rise from the dead. (Luke 16:31)

The resistance to the belief in Jesus' resurrection continues from that day to today when Muslims are not alone in their rejection of a crucified and risen Lord. Shortly after his leaving the gravecloths behind, Jesus' enemies seek to discredit the resurrection evidence (Matt. 28:11,12). There is already a religious sect of the Jews, the Sadducees, who reject any concept of a bodily resurrection (Matt. 22:23f). Paul argues against the reasoning of the Corinthians who oppose the idea of a physical resurrection of Jesus. "But in fact, Christ has been raised from the dead," he writes to convince some within the early church (1 Cor. 15:20).

Meditation: O Watcher of my Life, I recognize very feebly that the same power that brought up Your Son from the dead is available at all times to Your servant.

Deuteronomy 22:4 Amos 6:14 Habakkuk 2:7 Luke 2:34 Hebrews 11:35 Revelation 20:5

64 The Finder   اَلْوَاجِدُ AL-WĀJID

I have found David, my servant; with my holy oil I have anointed him; so that my hand shall ever abide with him. Psalm 89:20

The Holy One is not only a seeker and protector, he is also the one who finds those in every possible place and situation. The psalmist asks, "Whither shall I flee from thy presence?" The first part of the response is obvious: "If I ascend to heaven, thou art there!" The second part is more astounding: "If I make my bed in Sheol, thou art there!" (Ps. 139:7,8).

This name for God, Al-Wajid, does not appear in this form in the Hebrew Bible. But throughout scripture, the God who is the Seeker-Finder leads on to a fuller portrayal of God's faithful care over his creation. The theme of the Finder-God saturates the psalm of David quoted above.

> O Lord, thou has searched me and known me! Thou knowest when I sit down
> and when I rise up; thou discernest my thoughts from afar. (Ps. 139:1,23)

Any secret, unexplored life is an open book to our Creator God.

> For thou didst form my inward parts, thou didst knit me together in my mother's
> womb...Thy eyes beheld my unformed substance; in thy book were written,
> every one of them, the days that were formed for me. (139:13,16)

Along with the great poetry of the Hebrew Bible, the parables of Jesus are without peer in world religious literature. The story of the prodigal son is told in response to the murmurs of the Jewish legalists who complain, "This man receives sinners and eats with them" (Luke 15:2). Jesus tells them three different stories, beginning with the shepherd who lost one sheep. The second is about a woman who lost a coin. Both of these lost items are found and much elation follows. "Rejoice with me for I have found my sheep/coin which was lost," declares the shepherd/woman (6,9).

The stories continue with the lost son, but this one does not end with joy, even when the younger son finds himself in the far country among the hogs and returns home to a waiting father. The younger son is not recognized by the elder son, who clenches his teeth and makes an oblique reference to "a son of the father" but nothing about a returning brother (30). In the case of the sheep, it is one out of one hundred; for the coin, it is perhaps a set of ten; for the father it is one of two. The waiting father speaks through Jesus to the elder son and to the Jewish lawyers about his joy:

> It was fitting to make merry and be glad, for this your brother was dead, and is
> alive, he was lost, and is found. (32)

John the apostle refers to those whose names "were not found in the book of life" and who would therefore be "thrown into the lake of fire" (Rev. 20:15). Paul's earnest prayer is to be found in Christ, "not having a righteousness of my own based on law" (Phil. 3:9).

Meditation: My bountiful Lord, Your presence is mighty and Your hand is graciously offered. Your discernment is omnipresent to guide my will to holiness.

Genesis 6:8   2 Samuel 16:4   Proverbs 20:6   Matthew 7:7   John 4:25   Romans 7:21

99 Beautiful Names of God

66   The Unique One   أَلْوَاحِدُ AL-WĀHID

We beheld his glory, glory as the unique Son from the Father. John 1:14

Abraham's son Isaac was called his only (*yahid*) son three times in Genesis 22 (2,12,16). The elder son, Ishmael, offspring of Hagar and Abraham, was also his son; but because of Sarah and the intended sacrifice on Mt. Moriah, Isaac was the unique son. When the word appears in the Greek, *monogenas*, it takes on the meaning of "only" as well as "unique." The English, only begotten, is a faithful but not a helpful translation found in John 3:16 where "God so loved the world that he gave his only begotten son."

The uniqueness of Jesus the Messiah is tied closely to the root of the Hebrew word *yahid*, which means united. Jesus is united with God in a way that transformed the prophetic pronouncements regarding God's presence in the form of the Son of Man and the Son of God. The Hebrew prophets see the humble, suffering servant somehow united with the great messianic king. The virgin birth, as prophesied by Isaiah, foretold God's unique physical appearance among mortals:

> Lo, a virgin shall conceive and bear a son, and shall call his name, Immanuel, God with us. (Isa. 7:14 and Matt. 1:23)

The Gospel of Matthew does not let the fact escape that the son and his family spent time in Egypt, thus fulfilling the Exodus experiences and the words of Hosea 11:1.

Another unique characteristic of Jesus' ministry is his closeness to God whom he addresses as his Father. This provokes several confrontations with the Jewish establishment, like this one when they boast that "Abraham is their father":

> Jesus answers them, "If you were Abraham's children, you would do what Abraham did and...not seek to kill me....If God were your Father, you would love me, for I proceeded from God. (John 8:39f)

This closeness of Jesus Christ is broken only when he faces the cross and asks fervently that this shameful death be removed, not only because of its physical pain and humiliation, but because it separates Jesus, the obedient son, from his loving Father (Luke 22:42).

The Messianic message of the Son and Father relationship is unique because of the death and resurrection of the Son. The servant passages of Isaiah speak of the one who is "highly exalted" (52:13) and at the same time experiences the deprivations of a cruel time when he "poured out his soul to death" (53:12). The gospel records of four writers are in agreement that the death, burial and resurrection of Jesus Christ are actual events and that the faith of Christianity depends upon these events (John 20:30,31 and Luke 24:44f).

Paul the apostle opens his Roman letter with this hope:

> Jesus Christ is the designated Son of God in power, according to the Spirit of holiness by his resurrection from the dead. (1:4)

Meditation: You are the Expansive One, the Self-Creating One, who brings to Your servants new life through the gift of Jesus Christ to humankind.

Genesis 49:6   Psalm 86:11   Zechariah 12:10   John 17:11   Jude 25   Revelation 15:3

65 The Glorious, The Magnificent One   اَلْمَاجِدُ   **AL-MĀJID**

And Mary said, "My soul magnifies the Lord, and my spirit rejoices in God my Savior." Luke 1:47

The list of God's names returns to a familiar landscape of the majesty and glory of the almighty God. This name is a cognate of name number 48, Most Glorious, and, as such, is related to a rare Hebrew word that designates choice items of harvests and natural beauty (Deut. 33:13f). It is a favorite beautiful name for a child born in Arabic-speaking households.

The Hebrew word *gadol* was a useful synonym for Al-Majid elsewhere in the Bible. "Thy name will be magnified for ever,—The Lord of hosts is God over Israel" (2 Sam. 7:26). "Magnificent is the Lord!" was a praise often on the psalmist's lips (Ps. 35:27, 70:4). Solomon was praised by the Lord at his designation as King David's successor:

> The Lord gave Solomon great repute in the sight of all Israel, and bestowed upon him such magnificence as had not been on any king before him in Israel.
> (1 Chron. 29:25)

Nowhere is the glory of the Lord more on physical display than at the events surrounding the annunciation and birth of Jesus Christ. In the exalting lyrics of the Magnificat, the young Mary "magnifies the Lord" at the announcement by her cousin that Mary would be the mother of the Messiah (Luke 1:43f). The shepherds outside of Bethlehem are overcome by the "glory (*doxa*) of the Lord" (Luke 2:9). The Arabic Bible has the angelic host praising God at the birth of Jesus, "Glory (*al-majd*) to God in the highest and on earth peace among men with whom he is pleased" (2:14).

Mary is honored as the virgin mother of Jesus, not only throughout the Greek Bible and church history, but in several citations from the Qur'an, including this verse from Sura 3:45:

> The angels said to Maryam: "God bids you rejoice in tidings from him. His name is the Messiah, the son of Maryam. He shall be esteemed in this world and in the hereafter."

The Qur'an has Jesus denying for himself and for his mother any special adoration that would associate them with divinity (5:116f). Jesus' mother Mary plays an important role for Muslim mystics as a symbol of purity, yet she was impregnated by the Spirit of God. Her alleged tomb in Ephesus in Turkey draws both Muslim and Christian pilgrims from around the world.

John the apostle stands alongside Mary at the crucifixion of her Son, who speaks to them from the cross: "Woman, behold your son!" Then he turns to John and says, "Behold your mother!" John then takes Mary to his own home and perhaps to Asia Minor where they died (John 19:26,27). Jesus commends his followers earlier in the presence of his mother, Mary, and brothers, when he points out, "Whoever does the will of God is my brother, my sister, my mother" (Mark 3:35).

Meditation: O Glorious God, my Savior, join me with those virtuous holy ones, like Mary, who professed their faith in Your sovereignty and bountiful spirit without murmuring.

---

1 Chronicles 17:4 Zechariah 12:7 Psalm 138:2 Luke 9:26f Acts 10:46, 19:17

67 The One  AL-AHAD

Hear, O Israel: The Lord your God is one Lord. Deuteronomy 6:4

Both Arabic and Hebrew words are the same for this name for God, Al-Ahad. There is little disagreement on the nature of oneness among Muslims and Jewish believers who defend an absolute Oneness while Christians insist that Oneness belongs to the unique God, the Father, Son, and Holy Spirit. The development of the church teaching of God's mysterious unity, expressed as a Trinity, is an answer to the serious charge that Christians worship three gods. The Council of Nicaea responded in 325 A.D. that Jesus was nothing less than God incarnate (John 1:1), yet maintaining an uncompromising monotheism.

The Oneness of God, a truth that is fully integrated throughout the Hebrew scriptures, is expressed in the liturgy of Deuteronomy 6:4. The full weight of this Oneness can be seen in the English Bible when it reads God, the Holy (Al-Quddus, number 4). The word "one" does not appear in the original language, but the people of God understand that God is totally distinct from other gods and that he is the Holy (2 Kings 19:22, Ps. 89:18). The prophet Isaiah affirms this God, the Holy, more than any other writer in the Bible; but often it is affixed to God as "Redeemer" within his prophecies. "I will help you, says the Lord; your Redeemer is the Holy (One) of Israel" (41:14) and "Our Redeemer—the Lord of hosts is his name—is the Holy (One) of Israel" (47:4).

When the redemptive acts of God take place at the exodus from Egypt of the Israelite people under the prophet Moses, the uniqueness of God is reestablished by the giving of the law—"You shall have no other gods before me" (Ex. 20:3, Deut. 6:4). Two other writing prophets speak directly about the oneness of God just before the Messianic period. Zechariah prophesies of the coming epochs:

> And the Lord will become king over all the earth; on that day the Lord will be one and his name one. (Zech. 14:9)

Malachi provides the last Hebrew reference, prior to the New Covenant period, which reveals God as Father to the Jews of Judah.

> Have we not all one Father? Has not one God created us? Why then are we faithless to one another, profaning the covenant of our fathers? (Mal. 2:10)

Jesus Christ does nothing to distract from the central teaching of Deuteronomy 6:4 and commands his followers to do the same (Mark 12:29,32f). But Jesus introduces a new dynamic into the unique relationship when he persists in identifying his special ties to the Father as the Son and when he provokes his enemies by saying, "I and the Father are one" (John 10:30). The charges of blasphemy arise when he calls himself "Son of God" and hound him right up to his death on the cross (Luke 22:70).

Jesus prays that his disciples will not be alone when he departs from them, but that the Spirit will continue to be with them.

> The glory which thou has given me I give to them, that they may be one even as we are one. I in them and thou in me, that they may become perfectly one. (John 17:22,23)

Meditation: You alone are my God, without beginning, invisible, unbegotten, immortal, absolute in goodness and power. I so confess and more with all principalities and powers.

Numbers 15:16 Matthew 23:8-10 1 Corinthians 8:4,6 Galatians 3:20 Ephesians 4:5-8

68   The Eternal   الصَّمَدُ AS-SAMAD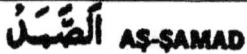

Abraham planted a tamarisk tree in Beersheba, and called on the name of the Lord, the Everlasting God. Genesis 21:33

The eternal nature of God is not a matter of disagreement within the family of Abrahamic faiths. The Qur'an uses this name one time (Sura 112:2); and an enhanced translation of As-Samad expands the two-word verse with this: "God the eternal, the uncaused cause of all that exists."[1] The Arabic, Hebrew and Greek Bibles do not use this name to describe God as eternal, preferring to use other terms that designate eternity, including a few words derived from Al-Baqi (number 96).

If this name of God comes from Hebrew terms, there are two possible sources for As-Samad: one with similar pronunciation meaning a yoked pair, and a second one with less linguistic association but more likely to have a related meaning. This second Hebrew word refers to foundation and establishment. "Thou didst set the earth on its foundation" (Ps. 104:5) is typical of this word's usage in the Bible.

In various poetical idioms, the foundation of the world is established on the seas (Ps. 24:2), by wisdom (Prov. 3:19) and laid out by the hand of the Lord (Isa. 48:13). The eternal God is pondered in this psalm:

> When I look at your heavens, the work of your fingers, the moon and the stars which you have established; what is man that you are mindful of him, and the son of man that you should care for him? (Ps. 8:3,4)

Linking this Hebrew word to the Eternal God is far easier than its other prominent use when it describes the transitory foundation of the temple of Solomon (2 Chron. 3:3) and the second temple at the time of Ezra (3:6) and Haggai (2:18).

The Greek Bible speaks of eternity by referring to the foundations of the world and by events connected with the end of time as we know it. These two concepts appear in the parable that Jesus told about the "blessed" inheriting the kingdom prepared for them "since the foundation of the world" (Matt. 25:34). Jesus' own words about eternal life and the accompanying judgment divide the "blessed" from those going to the "eternal fire" (Matt. 25:41f). Several other references to "the foundation of the world" appear in the final interpretations of the parables (Matt. 13:35), the glory of Christ (John 17:24), the election of his own blessed ones (Eph. 1:4 and 1 Peter 1:20) and the completion of the works of God (Heb. 4:3).

The words "everlasting" and "eternal" appear almost exclusively with the concept of life in the Greek Bible. John associates eternal life with gathering and harvesting "eternal" fruits (4:37); Paul proclaims that eternal life is a "gift from God" through Jesus Christ (Rom. 6:23); and the author of Hebrews speaks of the "eternal spirit" (9:14). Paul writes to Timothy, and other fellow servants, to do good and thus "lay up a good foundation for the future" (1 Tim. 6:19).

Meditation: Your kingdom is built on the sure foundation of Jesus Christ. O Redeemer, I confess that You are my eternal joy.

Genesis 17:13   Proverbs 10:25   Isaiah 28:16   1 Corinthians 3:1   Revelation 14:6

---

[1] Asad, p. 985.

69 All-Powerful, The Decreer  AL-QĀDIR

"Not by might, nor by power, but by my Spirit," says the Lord of hosts.
Zechariah 4:6

The subject of God's omnipotent strength persists throughout this list of the attributes of God. Al-Qadir and its close relative Al-Muqtadir (number 70) highlight the pre-existent power of God who is introduced by the biblical phrase, "before the foundations of the earth" (number 68). The subjects of the events that are known "before the foundations" of the world are limited in number and reveal future events that only God would know about in the course of "final things." There is no attempt to violate human volition and individual destinies regarding death, judgment day and ultimate positions in heaven, which are covered in very broad terms (Matt. 13:35, 25:34, John 17:24). The subject of predestination is never humanly resolved, as it assumes perfect knowledge of two contradictory phenomena — human freedom and God's sovereignty.

The Hebrew word *qadir*, indicating dark and dark things, provides little help in connecting this with God's decrees, powers and strength. God's decrees and ordinances are related to the name Al-Haqq (number 51) and are synonyms for law, statutes, and testimonies, which form part of the revelation and do not act as decrees or say anything that determines the future. God's power and might belong to other names such as numbers 8, 33, 37, 52, 53.

The Greek words that give credence to the concept of predestination are found in Paul's letter to the Romans:

> For those whom he foreknew he also predestined to be conformed to the image
> of his Son, in order that he might be the first-born among many brethren. (8:29)

This biblical reference, like the following one, is predictive of those destined for salvation; but it is nonspecific as to who falls into this category of being chosen, while saying nothing about those not selected. "God has not rejected his people whom he foreknew" serves to introduce the subject of God's grace in preserving the remnant of God's people for an ultimate purpose (Rom. 11:2).

In the Hebrew Bible, God has a long list of chosen persons who were elected, not on their merits, but for a purpose that was observed by the Mighty One alone. The list includes Abraham (Neh. 9:7), Moses and Aaron (Ps. 105:26), David (1 Sam. 10:24), and seed of Jacob (Ezek. 20:5). The Hebrew word does not exclude human choices, as mentioned in Isaiah 66:3 ("they have chosen their own ways") and Deuteronomy 30:19:

> I [the Lord] have set before you life and death, blessing and cursing; therefore
> choose life that you and your descendants will live.

The elect of God will enjoy special care, according to Matthew 24, which includes the promise that the chosen ones will be gathered from the "four winds, from one end of heaven to the other" (31).

Meditation: The night is still deep and dark, but Your dawn is approaching for Your righteous servants. I wait for You to dress me for the new day in the robes of Your blessedness.

Deuteronomy 12:11 1 Kings 11:13 Isaiah 65:9,22 Romans 8:33 2 Timothy 2:10 2 John 13

70   All-Powerful, The Determiner   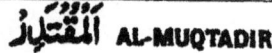 AL-MUQTADIR

And when the Gentiles heard [the good news] they were glad and glorified the word of God; and as many as were ordained to eternal life believed. Acts 13:48

Predestination, the subject of name number 69, continues with this name which is an emphatic form of the previous word. The name "the Determiner" is from Al-Ghazali who described the power that man possesses as "deficient...for he only attains some possibilities" of God's power.[1] The Hebrew Bible attests to unlimited power by its confession of the following divine attributes: the All-Knowing (number 19), the Wise (46), the First and the Last (73,74). God as the Predestinator receives attention in both the Hebrew and Greek sections of the Bible, but nothing is similar to the emphasis of Sura 97, which is among the earliest chapters in the Qur'an:

> Lo! from on high we brought down this on the night of destiny. What can we say about the night of destiny! The night of destiny is better than a thousand months.

Among the cardinal beliefs of Muslims is Qadir—Doctrine of Foreordination, the Decrees of God, God's Will. The Qur'an itself has several verses that seem to indicate God offers freedom to his subjects (2:286 and 18:28), but the overwhelming impact is for God's determined sovereignty over all human choices. "This is the reminder to all humankind, to all of you who choose the straight path, but you will not choose, except God the Lord of the world" (81:27-29). God's *qadar* extends to his own words, according to Sura 2:106:

> Whatever verse we may annul or cause you to forget, we will bring a better one than it, or one like it; do you not know that God has power (*qadir*) over all things?

The Christian theologian George Adam Smith cites the call of Jeremiah when he was in his mother's womb (Jer. 1:5) as an analogy for understanding biblical predestination:

> It is not to character or fate, to salvation and its opposite, to eternal life or eternal punishment, but to service, or some particular form of service, for God and man.[2]

The servant of the Lord in Isaiah is designated to speak for justice:

> Lo, my servant, whom I uphold, my chosen, in whom my soul delights; I have put my Spirit upon him, he will bring forth justice to the nations. (Isa. 42:1)

The sermon of the apostle Peter in the Jerusalem temple precinct declares the service which Christ performed for all.

> "This Jesus, delivered up according to the definite plan and foreknowledge of God, you crucified and killed by the hands of lawless men. But God raised him up, having loosed the pangs of death, because it was not possible for him to be held by it. (Acts 2:23,24)

Meditation: Let me never forget that I am ever with You, O compassionate One.

Deuteronomy 17:15   Job 15:5   Proverbs 8:10,19   Matthew 24:22   1 Peter 2:6

---

[1] Al-Ghazali, p. 131.

[2] George Adam Smith, *Jeremiah: The Baird Lecture for 1922*, 4th ed. (New York: Harper and Brothers, n.d.), p. 336.

71 The One Who Advances, The Expediter   ٱلْمُقَدِّمُ   AL-MUQADDIM

He is the head of the body...the beginning, the first-born from the dead, that in everything he might be preeminent. Colossians 1:18

The root of this name for God's foundational work in his creation originates from a single Semitic root that flourishes today in multiple Arabic and Hebrew words. Al-Muqaddim doubles with the next name, Al-Mu'akhkhir, to reveal the range of God's activities from the point of view of time. The most basic use of this word, however, means to come before, which is not related to time. The prophet asks, "With what shall I come before the Lord?" He repeats, "Shall I come before him with burnt offerings?" (Mic. 6:6).

This name moves away from closeness in space to distance in time, which is part of its Hebrew usage. "The Lord created me at the beginning of his work, the first of his acts (*qadam*) of old" (Prov. 8:22). David's kingly praises include this word of thanks to his Lord: "He asked life of thee; thou gavest it to him, length of days for ever and ever" (Ps. 21:4). A synonym for this word for ancient is used to define the messianic character of Daniel's night vision:

> I saw...with the clouds of heaven there came one like a son of man, and he came to the Ancient of Days and was presented before him. (Dan. 7:13)

The prophet describes the coming of the Ancient of Days who will set up judgments with the holy ones (*qaddishi*) (7:22). Jesus Christ identifies with this setting of his returning to earth as the Son of Man. He uses apocalyptic language to indicate the expansiveness of the universal gospel (Matt. 24:27). Jesus promises his disciples that "all tribes on earth will mourn, and they will see the Son of man coming in the clouds of heaven with power and great glory" (24:30).

The Revelation of John (1:7) speaks about this theme of the coming of Christ in the clouds within eyesight of all, and adds the words of the prophet Zechariah:

> When they shall look on him whom they have pierced, they shall mourn for him, as one mourns for an only child, and weep for him, as one weeps over a first-born. (12:10)

The honored position of the first-born son is part of the name that Jesus assumed at the scene of the virgin birth recorded in Matthew and Luke. "She gave birth to her first-born son" (Luke 2:7). His coming to the earth in the first instance culminates in his death and resurrection, which are precipitous events for all believers. For Paul, Jesus Christ is "the first-born of all creation" and of the resurrection (Col. 1:15,18). The early followers of Jesus are addressed by Paul as the "first fruits of the Spirit" (Rom. 8:23). James' call to fellow believers and servants to live up to their calling as "first fruits" is a precursor of greater things to follow (James 1:18).

Meditation: O Matchless One, You are before all things and You have trusted me to believe in You.

Psalm 143:5   Jonah 4:2,8   Ezekiel 16:55,56   Mark 13:4   Romans 8:29

99 Beautiful Names of God

72 The Delayer, The Postponer  AL-MU'AKHKHIR

And it shall come to pass in the latter days that the mountain of the house of the Lord shall be established...and all the nations shall flow to it, and many peoples will come.
Isaiah 2:2,3

The previous word, al-muqaddim, which contrasts with this name for God, has similar Hebrew and Arabic words, as does this present name. There are broad meanings for this word in the two modern languages, as is the case for the Bible background of Al-Mu'akhkhir. The religious use refers to the latter days, as is the case for the Isaiah verse above; but the word itself is based upon the ordinary word for "last" (number 74).

While Al-Muqaddim looks to the God of the beginnings, of the ancient times and as the first fruits, this name, Al-Mu'akhkhir, surveys the future and what is considered last in human time. The words are used to denote direction with *qadam*, indicating the area east of Jerusalem or facing the rising sun (Ezek. 11:1). Al-Mu'akhkhir is identified with directions toward the west (Deut. 11:24, Job 18:20). In the Gospels, Jesus speaks of events in the coming days that will draw many "from east and west" to "sit at table with Abraham, Isaac, and Jacob in the kingdom of heaven" (Matt. 8:11, Luke 13:29).

The Second Epistle of Peter defines a delaying God, with this general warning about forbearance:

> But do not ignore this ..., beloved, that with the Lord one day is as a thousand years, and a thousand years as one day. The Lord is not slow about his promise as some count slowness, but is forbearing toward you, not wishing that any should perish, but that all should reach repentance. (3:8,9)

A form of this name appears in the Qur'an where scoffers are asking the Lord about judgment: "Why is it delayed?" (Sura 11:8).

Another phrase that conveys the patient mercy of God in the Bible is found in the expression, "The Lord repented." The term describes a period of time for God to withhold judgment on the sinful created world. When God is set to destroy the earth, he finds and saves Noah and his family and destroys the earth later (Gen. 6:7). The Lord does not immediately respond by destroying the Israelites for building the golden calf, but delays it until Moses and Aaron are able to take an account of the faithfulness of some (Ex. 32:14). In the turbulent days of Jeremiah, the prophet pleads with the people to repent and wait for God to repent. They refuse and judgment falls on the city of Jerusalem (Jer. 26:3f).

In each of these incidents from the Hebrew Bible, a remnant remains after the larger groups are destroyed. The believers in the true God treasure this promise in the days of moral and political anarchy: "For out of Jerusalem shall go forth a remnant, and out of Mount Zion a band of survivors" (2 Kings 19:31).

Paul reminds his Roman readers that Elijah survived with seven thousand others who did not bow down to the false gods. "So, too, at the present time there is a remnant, chosen by grace" (Rom. 11:5).

Meditation: By Your generous love, light up my path in this world that will safely move me forward to the next.

Genesis 24:56 1 Kings 14:10 Amos 7:3,6 Luke 12:45 Romans 9:27 Revelation 11:13

73 The First  AL-AWWAL

I am the first and I am the last; besides me there is no god. Isaiah 44:6

A wise teacher was asked, "How do you know God?" He responded, "Through the fact that he brings opposites together."

The Sufi mystic Ibn Arabi identifies the Ancient of Days with this name for God because he is without beginnings.[1] These beautiful names of God (71-74) demonstrate God's timelessness from the "beginning to the end" when there is neither end nor beginning. Al-Awwal complements number 71 and is in opposition to numbers 72 and 74.

The Hebrew uses several words for first, which include the word for One (number 67) and the word for head, *rashon*. God is the Head of the priests in the order of battle (2 Chron. 13:12). The Greek Bible gives the name of the first and last letters in the alphabet to show the vastness of God's mercy and power.

"I am the Alpha and the Omega," says the Lord God, who is and who was and who is to come, the Almighty. (Rev. 1:8)

The earliest gospel was written by Mark, who was a young man when Jesus was with the disciples. Mark depended heavily on the apostle Peter for sources of his Gospel, but he did introduce himself into the narrative rather immodestly when he was stripped by the mob at the pre-crucifixion trials (Mark 14:51,52). Mark's Gospel moves rapidly to show that Jesus is the Son of God to his largely non-Jewish readers. The Gospel of Mark begins, "At the beginning of the gospel, the Son of God" (1:1). The selection of events for this Gospel is based upon vivid actions on the part of Jesus, especially his interaction with Peter and the other disciples.

When Jesus appeared with Moses and Elijah on the mountaintop, Mark noted the marvelous conclusion when the two former prophets disappeared and the disciples saw "Jesus only" (9:8). The scenes in Mark change quickly, but the narrative pauses often when children are involved. Jesus invites a child into the inner circle of his followers to make the point, "If anyone would be first, he must be last of all and servant of all" (9:35). "Whoever causes one of these little ones who believes in me to sin," Jesus spoke later to his disciples, "it would be better for him if a millstone were hung round his neck and he were thrown into the sea" (9:42).

Days later, Mark records Jesus' rebuking the disciples when they try to turn children away: "Truly I say to you, whoever does not receive the kingdom of God like a child shall not enter it" (10:15). Again, directing his words to his disciples, Jesus warns them, "Children, how hard it is to enter the kingdom of God" (10:24). Jesus summarizes what he considers first for his followers—to leave one's family, children and lands for the sake of the gospel. Any persecution for the kingdom will be rewarded in the "age to come" (10:30). The message again is, "But many that are first will be last, and the last first" (10:31).

Meditation: My Jesus, Your emphasis on the reversal of firsts and lasts for the sake of the gospel is an irritant in modern life. I seek Your Spirit's wisdom in making the choices for Your kingdom.

Genesis 1:5 Deuteronomy 26:2 Psalm 139:16 Matthew 17:10,11 Romans 2:9,10

---

[1] Ibn Arabi, p. 55.

74 The Last  AL-ĀKHIR

To the messenger of the church in Smyrna write: "The words of the first and the last, who died and came to life." Revelation 2:8

In the Scriptures, the word "last" applies to every-day events, but it also refers to a transcendent reality in the future, especially referring to situations when there is nothing to follow. One of the earliest concerns beyond this life is found in Job's remarkable affirmation, "I know that my Redeemer lives and at last he will stand upon the earth" (19:25). The Song of Moses reminded the Israelite tribes, "If they were wise, they would understand this, they would discern their latter end" (Deut. 32:29). Isaiah mocks the people speaking to their idols, "Tell us what is to come hereafter, that we may know that you are gods" (Isa. 41:23).

The close association between this word in Arabic and Hebrew is discussed under name 72 which is derived from Al-Akhir. The Greek New Testament introduces into the language of Christians the word eschatology, which was based on the word *eschatos*, last. The Qur'an uses *al-akhira* to signify the hereafter, the final eschatological scenes. Sura 3:45 refers to "The Messiah, son of Mary, honored in this world and in the hereafter." An earlier sura devotes several thoughts about the Qur'anic "last things" which include a three-way division after death and judgment. The first division includes those who did what was right, the second did evil, but the "foremost" were those who were drawn close to God (by doing good works) and only "a few" will be in this group to fully occupy the heavenly gardens (Sura 56:7f).

Jesus speaks to his disciples about the narrow way that leads to life "and those who find it are few" (Matt. 7:14), and he warns of the time when there will be separation of the blessed and those "cast into outer darkness." Jesus repeats, "For many are called, but few are chosen" (Matt. 22:13,14). Jesus Christ's strongest words of condemnation are directed at those who live double lives, hypocrites, who are concerned about external appearances, but inside their souls they are like "whitewashed tombs" (Matt. 23:27). He speaks of judgment, hell, rewards, and heaven throughout his public ministry, but he prefaces his remarks with this challenging teaching:

> I tell you, unless your righteousness exceeds that of the scribes and Pharisees, you will never enter the kingdom of heaven. (Matt. 5:20)

Jesus' promise of the *Paraclete*, the Holy Spirit, was to help his followers remain faithful in the world once Jesus had departed from them.

> When he [the Paraclete] comes, he will convince the world of sin and of righteousness and of judgment. (John 16:8)

For Peter, the last days begin at the feast of Pentecost with the coming of the Holy Spirit, who will be followed by greater eschatological events, according to Acts 2:17f. Before the great and manifest final day of the Lord comes, the apostle declares, "Whoever calls on the name of the Lord shall be saved" (2:20,21).

Meditation: Comfort me with the words that You are always with me even to the end, O Redeemer and Savior.

Isaiah 59:16, 65:12   Micah 4:1   John 6:40,44   1 Corinthians 15:8,26,45   1 John 2:18

75 The Manifest 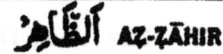 AZ-ZĀHIR

All nations shall come and worship thee, for thy judgments have been made manifest.
Revelation 15:4

The Bible's rich vocabulary provides suitable substitutes for this common Arab word, translated often as visible, apparent, appearance. Az-Zahir has the closest affinity with a Hebrew word that means noon, midday, symbol of brightness, and is found in the prophecies of Daniel, where the Aramaic is translated:

> Those who are wise shall shine like the brightness of the firmament; and those who turn many to righteousness, like the stars for ever and ever. (12:3)

There is a strong ethical association between enlightenment and concern for the hungry and the afflicted. Isaiah states, "If you pour yourself out for the hungry and satisfy the desire of the afflicted, then shall your light rise in the darkness" (Isa. 58:10). A psalm of Asaph opens with a prayer to the Shepherd of Israel and continues to cry out, "You who are enthroned upon the cherubim, shine forth" (Ps. 80:1).

The Lord God uses various methods to show his people his mighty glory. Often God appears in dreams, as is the case with Joseph and the pharaoh (Gen. 41) and Daniel with the king of Babylon (Dan. 2:6). Moses tells his people to "stand firm and watch the salvation (*yashu'*) of the Lord that will work for you in overpowering the Egyptians" (Ex. 14:13). Psalm 147:19 praises God for manifesting his word to Jacob, "his statutes and ordinances to Israel." More than any other disclosure of himself, God shows his mercy (*rahum*) to many of his servants, including David (Ps. 18:50), and lovingkindness (*hesed*) to thousands (Jer. 32:18).

The Greek Bible, like its Hebrew counterpart, has a rich vocabulary that reveals God's openness toward his creation. Paul's letter to his fellow servant Titus bursts forth with a string of descriptions of the most explicit God:

> God, who never lies, promised ages ago and at the proper time manifested in his word through the preaching with which I have been entrusted by command of God our Savior. (Titus 1:2,3)

The second letter sent by Paul to Timothy, his companion in ministry, is likewise filled with joy for the visitation of God's grace in former times and which is "now manifested through the appearing of our Savior Christ Jesus" (1:10).

While Jesus takes time to explain himself carefully to his twelve disciples, there are instances when they do not understand his full mission as he has only three years to spend with them. He does answer Philip, when he asks, "Lord, show us the Father." Jesus' response is a question for Philip, "Do you not believe that I am in the Father and the Father in me?" (John 14:10).

Within days, Jesus is speaking again to his disciples about his closeness to God his Father. He promises them the Spirit of truth who will come to his own and manifest and glorify the Son and the Father (John 16:13f). Jesus explains earlier the Spirit's proceeding from the Father and that this Counselor/Paraclete "will bear witness to me" and reminds them that they are witnesses to manifest his truth (15:26f).

Meditation: Let Your divine light shine on me and keep me in Your Spirit's loving gaze.

Genesis 24:12 Numbers 16:5 Psalm 16:11 John 16:13 Acts 1:3 1 Peter 1:7

76 The Inner, The Hidden   ٱلْبَاطِنُ AL-BĀTIN

Call to me and I will answer, and will tell you great and hidden things which you have not known. Jeremiah 33:3

The pairing of this name with the previous name, the Manifest One, reveals the inclusiveness of the Lord God who occupies all times and all spaces. Human beings are richly endowed with both of these characteristics, enjoying physical "appearances" and inner, spiritual qualities. All human spirits are subject to the body of flesh that forces men and women to be tired, irritable, and eventually to die. But the human spirit has the wonderful quality which enables it to rise above the material and temporal worlds. Believers in Christ, who are led by the Holy Spirit, may call out to the Father, as infant sons and daughters learning to speak, cry, "Abba! Baba! Papa." Paul continues this theme in Romans.

> It is the Spirit himself bearing witness with our spirit that we are children, then heirs,...fellow heirs of Jesus Christ, provided we suffer with him. (8:15,16)

The inner person is the subject of many of Jesus' talks with his followers and they, along with his detractors, are often confounded by what he says in direct and parabolic statements. He tells the legalists, the Pharisees, that the kingdom of God's presence can not be observed in one place and not in another: "For behold, the kingdom of God is in the midst of you" (Luke 17:21). Mark's Gospel presents a shorter form of a parable about the seed that was planted and eventually produced a harvest from the stalk of wheat.

The kingdom of God is a process that, like a growing seed, cannot be observed, even if the farmer goes out in the middle of the night to see it grow. However, the growth of that grain may be seen in these stages: the blade, then the ear, then the full grain in the ear (Mark 4:26). This short narrative is part of just a few words of Jesus that appear in the Qur'an where there is an interpretation of the stages of growth identifying the Torah and the Gospel with the seed and the blade respectively (Sura 48:29f).

The Hebrew word for Al-Batin is first a name for the belly, body, womb, in the physical sense, and later it becomes the name for the inner, unobserved workings of the body. The pronunciation is similar in both Arabic and Hebrew. Job describes his physical birth from his mother's womb (3:10) while the psalmist asserts that the body as the *batin* is in contrast to the soul (31:9). The proverb tells of the words of a whisperer "that go down into the inner parts of the body" (Prov. 18:8). The hiddenness of God is represented by Hebrew words other than Al-Batin, which are observed in this revelation to Moses:

> And God said to Moses, "I am the Lord. I appeared to Abraham, to Isaac, to Jacob as God, *El Shaddai*, but by my name the Lord I did not make myself known to them." (Ex. 6:2,3)

Throughout the scriptures, the Most High is continually inviting his faithful ones to draw near to him, just as Moses approaches the burning bush and meets God in an intimate way (Ex. 3:13). Paul meets the sophisticated Athenians gathered around an idol dedicated to the unknown God, and calls upon the polytheists to worship "the God who made the world and everything in it" (Acts 17:22f).

Meditation: Though I would understand all of Your mysterious ways, if I have not love, I am nothing.

Numbers 16:22   Psalm 91:1   Matthew 13:10   Romans 8:1-9   1 Peter 3:4,5

77 The Governor, The Ruler — اَلْوَالِي AL-WĀLI

Come and see what God has done...who rules by his might for ever, whose eyes keep watch on the nations. Psalm 66:5,7

The teaching of the kingdom of God is the central theme in Jesus' ministry, which he extended to a prayer he taught his followers to pray. "Thy kingdom come, thy will be done, on earth as it is in heaven" (Matt. 6:10). The emphasis, even in this prayer, is the spiritual linkage between the pray-ers and their spiritual Father; yet there is allowance for the more earthly rule that is often forgotten when the prayer is directed toward the rule of the heavenly One. The name Al-Wali bears witness that God is the over-all Ruler, the absolute King of his creation—this world and all other worlds.

Al-Ghazali defines this name more precisely for fellow Muslims:

> So there is no ruler over things except God...He is, first of all, the sole planner; secondly the one who implements the plan by realizing it.[1]

Al-Wali appears only in Arabic, but the Hebrew and the Greek Bibles are not lacking in proper terms for rule. "Kingdom" was the prominent word in both Testaments; but other names, as suggested by this list of the 99 names so far, are apparent in the Bible. (Refer to King: number 3; Just: 29; Trustee: 52; Powerful: 53; Equitable: 86, for a fuller idea of what is considered God's just and powerful rule and how this is interpreted in human experiences.)

The first records of human rule for the people of God are calls for God's direct rule either through his priests and their interpretation of the law (Ex. 19:6), or an attempt to make God king in Jeshurun (Deut. 33:4,5). Both types of theocracies fail as the tribes settle in the promised land. The period of the judges allows the Israelites a tribal confederacy that rules with only minor successes. One of the judges, Gideon, turns down an inherited rule for his son by insisting, "I will not rule over you or my son will not rule. The Lord will rule over you" (Judg. 8:23).

The most enduring government is the monarchy which reaches its zenith under David and Solomon; but that is followed by a break into a kingdom in Judah and a northern kingdom called Israel. During the long period of decline, the Davidic kingdom becomes a metaphor for a return to a stable rule for the nation.

The great writing prophets each see David's throne restored with some possibilities of a combined divine-human rule over the earth. Isaiah sees David's kingdom coming with "justice and righteousness" (9:7), while Ezekiel envisions David as king, shepherd, and servant who would bring a "covenant of peace to the nations" (37:24f).

Jesus warns his followers that the example of the Gentile world where authority and government are abused would not be the rule for his kingdom, where "whoever would be great among you must be your servant" (Mark 10:42-45).

Meditation: Hear the prayers of Your people who suffer under unjust rulers.

Genesis 14,17,18   Psalm 66:7   Matthew 1:20   John 3:1   Romans 13   Hebrews 11:33

---

[1] Al-Ghazali, p. 140.

99 Beautiful Names of God

78 The Highest One   المتعالي AL-MUTA'ALI

The Most High rules the kingdom of men, and gives it to whom he will. Daniel 4:25

This name is built upon name number 36, the Most High, and its association with the Hebrew is strong. Al-Muta'ali appears only once in the Qur'an (Sura 13:9) where God is described as far above any thoughts of his creatures. The Book of Daniel provides a good look at this word in the Bible.

The Most High God's name first appears in Daniel's prophecy in the Aramaic language when the Babylonian King Nebuchadnezzar calls out the names of the three Hebrews who were tossed into the fiery furnace for refusing to bow to the golden idol.

"Shadrach, Meshach, and Abednego, servants of the Most High God, come forth, and come here!" (Dan. 3:26)

The king issues an edict to his pagan kingdom that the God of the three Hebrew youths would be accepted as one of the gods of the Babylonians (3:28f). Later this great king's son, Belshazzar, summons Daniel to interpret the mysterious writing that appeared on the wall of the royal banquet hall. Before Daniel successfully provides the interpretation of the four words, he addresses King Belshazzar, "O King, the Most High God gave Nebuchadnezzar your father kingship, greatness and majesty." Then Daniel recounts the degrading disease of Nebuchadnezzar when he acted insanely, "eating grass like an ox." This lasted until "he knew that the Most High God rules the kingdom of men, and sets over it whom he wills" (5:21).

The name, Most High, reappears in the seventh chapter of the book where the visions of future events are unfolded: "The Most High shall receive the kingdom and possess it for ever" (7:18). The name occurs with the apocalyptic idiom "Ancient of Days" in the vision in 7:22. A great, ten-horned beast who arrogantly challenges the Most High is presented:

He [the fourth beast] shall speak words against the Most High, and shall wear out the saints of the Most High, and shall think to change the times and the law; for a time, two times, and a half a time. (7:25)

Daniel, a late Hebrew prophet, is a transitional character in the biblical canon. His book is one of the most autobiographical in the Bible, yet there are widely divergent opinions on the historical events that are covered in his writings. His name abounds throughout his own text, which, along with Ezra, was written in Aramaic. The prophet Ezekiel refers to Daniel's joining with the prophets Noah and Job as men of God who can not stay the judgment of God upon the house of Israel (Ezek. 14:14,20). Jesus names the prophet Daniel as the source of the prophecy regarding the pending destruction of Jerusalem (Matt. 24:15).

The Babylonian king, Nebuchadnezzar, (Dan. 3:26) had one thing in common with a man possessed with a demon (Mark 5:7) and a cultic slave girl in the Roman city of Philippi (Acts 16:16,17). These were non-Jews who recognized the Most High God.

Meditation: Height, width, depth and breadth, all dimensions of inner and outer space are Your spaces, O my Compassionate Savior.

Genesis 14:19   Job 38:18   Psalm 82:6   Lamentations 3:35,38   Hebrews 7:1

99 Beautiful Names of God

79 The Righteous, The Pure  AL-BARR

The fear of the Lord is clean, enduring for ever. Psalm 19:9

Al-Barr takes the usual route from early Hebrew concrete terms defining shining and polished arrows to the more transcendent terms describing a pure and righteous God. Arabic and Hebrew pronunciations and meanings are almost identical. The basic Greek Bible word, *katharos*, indicates that the word had special ceremonial uses in washing and burial customs. However, the biblical word for righteous, doing good, and godly took forms other than *barr*, which the Arabic Bible retains for special reverence for God.

The prophets Isaiah and Jeremiah speak of polished arrows. Isaiah sees himself as one "hid in a quiver," referring to his mother's womb (Isa. 49:2). Jeremiah's reference point is a call to battle—"Sharpen the arrows!" (51:11). The term takes on liturgical meanings elsewhere in the Scriptures. Clean vessel carriers in Isaiah (52:11), musicians (1 Chron. 16:41) and sheep (Neh. 5:18) connect it to the temple services. These servants, Job (33:3), David (Ps. 24:4) and Zephaniah (3:9) call on the High God to clean their tongues, hands, hearts, and lips as they prepare for worship.

Jesus surprises his disciples by taking on the role of a servant and washing the feet of the Twelve who meet with him just hours before his betrayal. Peter at first refuses to see his Master in such a humiliating position, but Jesus prevails when he says to this inner circle of friends, "He who has bathed does not need to wash, except for his feet"; then he adds an enigmatic statement regarding his betrayal by the disciple Judas, "But not all of you are clean" (John 13:11).

Jesus Christ has several exchanges with his enemies about the necessity of external washing. One time he is challenged by the legalists for not washing his hands before dinner. He charges them,

"Now you Pharisees cleanse the outside of the cup and of the dish, but inside you are full of extortion and evil." (Luke 11:39)

A similar exchange is reported about clean hands and utensils, which evokes this response by Jesus when he quotes Isaiah (29:13): "This people honors me with their lips, but their heart is far from me" (Mark 7:6).

Baptism, a ceremonial washing that some of the Jews accept for themselves and for converts, Jesus does not condemn, and actually receives baptism himself by John the Baptist (Matt. 3:1-13). The rite is accompanied by "confession of sins" (3:6). Water baptism is intended to be a precursor to the baptism of the Holy Spirit which originally took place on the day of Pentecost, according to Acts 1:5,6 and 2:1-21. The apostle Paul responds to the invitation to be baptized when he first becomes a believer (Acts 22:16). He later writes that the body of believers, the Church, is redeemed and made holy by Christ, and "cleansed" by the "washing of water with the word" (Eph. 5:25,26).

Meditation: There is no other righteousness, save what You have provided for me. Keep my inner life pure, O Loving Redeemer.

Job 11:24 Psalm 2:12 Matthew 5:8 2 Corinthians 6:8 2 Timothy 4:8 Revelation 22:14

80 Accepter of Repentance, Ever-Relenting 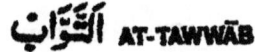 AT-TAWWĀB

Do you not know that God's goodness is meant to lead you to repentance? Romans 2:4

This beautiful name for God suggests some interesting Hebrew cognates that help define the Arabic word, At-Tawwab, God the one who leads to repentance. The Bible does not back away from the idea that God repents; and both Hebrew and Greek words can express this (cf. number 72). This name for God, At-Tawwab, does not appear in the Scriptures; yet by looking at minor changes of the consonants in this name, two very widely used Hebrew words emerge. J. Windrow Sweetman suggests that both *towb* (good) and *showb* (return, repent) are the closest Hebrew words for this attribute of the High God.[1]

God is good. The etymology of our English word for good from God's name indicates how the name and attribute are bound together in European languages. From Genesis 1:4, where God declared his creation good (towb), to one of the last Greek testament books, 3 John 11, "imitate good," the words for good abound throughout the holy Scriptures. Psalm 34 picks up themes that appear elsewhere—God is good and worthy of trust (v. 8), those who follow God "will lack no good thing" (10), they will enjoy life with good days (12), and they should "do good and seek peace" (14).

Jesus uses an opportunity to teach about the good God in a conversation he had with a very religious man, who ends up walking away after Jesus directed him: "Go, sell what you have, and give to the poor" (Mark 10:21). This observant Jew is unable to turn away from his possessions. The importance of the word *showb* in the Bible is shown when Jesus begins his public ministry with the cry, "Repent, the kingdom of heaven is at hand" (Matt. 3:2). The message of the evangelists Peter (Acts 2:38) and Paul (17:30), and John's messages to the churches of Asia Minor (Rev. 2:5, 3:19) all invite their listeners to repent.

In the Hebrew Bible, among those who call upon the people to return to God were the prophets Hosea (7:10), Amos (4:6) and Jeremiah (3:7). The Lord God was often the subject of repentance; this provokes a rigorous discussion between the prophet Samuel and King Saul when Samuel surmises that the glorious God "is not a man that he should repent" (1 Sam. 15:29). However, God is on record for changing his mind, or postponing judgments, as were the appeals of Noah (Gen. 6:7), Jonah (3:9), and Daniel (9:6). The prophet Zechariah offers this hope, "Thus says the Lord of hosts, Return unto me...and I will return to you" (1:3).

The two instances in the Qur'an where God is called At-Tawwab are translated by one commentator "For he is Oft-Returning"[2] (2:37 and 2:54). One of the last suras in the Qur'an is named "Repentance," At-Tawbah (9), and offers repentance to those who have turned their hearts away from the faith (27 and 110). This sura assails the two peoples of the book, Jews and Christians, for the sin of *shirk*, making partners of God (30 and 31). Shirk adherents face a severe judgment, according to Sura 98:6.

Meditation: Your wonderful words offering forgiveness and repentance to me are my living hope.

Exodus 32:12 Judges 21:6 2 Kings 23:26 Jeremiah 26:3 Luke 17:3 Romans 7:8

---

[1] Sweetman, vol. 1, p. 19.

[2] Ali, pp. 26, 30.

81 The Avenger  AL-MUNTAQIM

O Lord, thou God of vengeance, thou God of vengeance, shine forth! Psalm 94:1

The subject of God's dishonoring and debasing returns with this name, but instead of a single merciful name in response to this severe name, this attribute of God is surrounded by two words, numbers 80, Accepter of Repentances, and 82, the Pardoner, revealing his all-encompassing compassion. God speaks singularly with myriads of voices. The human ear picks up only one or two voices of God, namely to recognize "that power belongs to God and that to thee, O Lord, belongs steadfast love (*hesed*)" (Ps. 62:11).

The Bible is clear that the attribute of avenging belongs to the Creator God and restricts human vengeance. We have the cry of the psalmist to God reminding him to powerfully strike back at those who are "wicked" (Ps. 94:3) and "arrogant boasters" (4). The psalmist asks those who are expecting immediate justice, "He who chastens the nations, does he not chastise?" (10). The Arabic name Al-Muntaqim is a close facsimile to the Hebrew word in this psalm.

At the close of the reading of the law of God, prior to crossing into the promised land, the prophet Moses breaks into song. Twice within this beautiful hymn of praise to the bountiful God, the subject of vengeance occurs. "Vengeance is mine" (Deut. 32:35) is repeated several times in the Bible. The second reference within Moses' song provides definite hope of the Lord's retribution on behalf of his servants.

> Praise his people, O you nations; for he avenges the blood of his servants, and takes vengeance on his adversaries. (Deut. 32:43)

The threat of God's visitation of anger hangs over the Levitical priests for not walking according to the path of God's commandments. "I will smite you sevenfold," he warns in Leviticus 26:23f. Earlier he forbids vengeance within the Israelite people.

> You shall not take vengeance or bear any grudge against the sons of your own people, but you shall love your neighbor as yourself; I am the Lord. (Lev. 19:18)

God's vengeance is directed against the Babylonian-Chaldean people (Isa. 47:3), against the evil practices in Jerusalem (Jer. 5:9) and against the sins of Judah (Jer. 9:9).

Jesus commends his followers for not seeking retribution when he tells them, "If anyone strikes on the right cheek, turn to him the other also" (Matt. 5:39). Paul, following in the steps of the risen Lord and Messiah, gives instructions concerning not repaying evil for evil (Rom. 12:17).

> Beloved, never avenge yourselves, but leave it to the wrath of God; for it is written, "Vengeance is mine, I will repay, says the Lord." (12:19)

According to the instructions to the Christians in Rome, the proper instrument on earth to administer justice is what Paul describes as "governing authorities" (13:1-5). Obeying those in authority is an important feature in understanding God who has delegated powers to the civil authorities, who are also "servants of God" and are to "execute wrath on the wrong-doer" (13:4).

Meditation: I wait for Your justice with all of Your creation. Meanwhile, I trust You to see me securely through this life where injustices are widely practiced, O my living One.

Genesis 4:15 Judges 11:36 Proverbs 6:34 Isaiah 47:3 Mark 14:47f Revelation 19:2

82   The Pardoner   اَلْعَفُوّ AL-'AFUW

For you, O Lord, are good and forgiving, abounding in steadfast love to all who call on you. Psalm 86:5

    Proceeding from the two opening names, Ar-Rahman and Ar-Rahim, and the two names identified with Al-Ghaffar, 14 and 34, this word joins with the next one (83), the Compassionate, in expressing God as the gracious forgiver. While this name is not found in the Hebrew Bible in this form, the idea of a pardoning, sustaining God is clearly apparent there. The suggestion that this word deals with minor infractions comes from reading the Bible legal codes; and the use of this word in modern Arabic functions about the same as an English "Excuse me." This is offset by the words of the psalmist who moans, "Lord, pardon my guilt for it is great!" (Ps. 25:11).

    An Israelite was bound to make an offering for touching an unclean object, according to Leviticus 5:10 where a burnt offering is accepted by the priest. After the priest makes "atonement for him for the sin which he has committed...he shall be forgiven." The sin and guilt offerings depend on several matters, like the weight of the offense and how much the sinner could afford to pay for restitution.

    During the decline of the kingdoms of Judah and Israel, the prophet Amos mocks the religious practices connected with keeping the precise numbers of sins, pardons, and punishments. Amos, who was a keen observer of human nature, introduces his prophecy with a parody of how far evil has advanced not only among the surrounding nations but in the very soul of his people. The chant-like cadence begins, "For three transgressions and for four," and was repeated concerning Damascus, Gaza, Tyre, Edom, Ammon, and Moab. Judah is accused of rejecting the law and not keeping the ordinances (Amos 2:4). The full weight of God's punishment will fall upon Israel, however. The word of God continues:

> For three transgressions and for four, I will not revoke the punishment; because they sell the righteous for silver and the needy for a pair of shoes. (Amos 2:6)

    The remaining prophecies in this small book within the Hebrew Bible are filled with God's gracious offers to pardon the people for their gross sins; but in the end judgment will come when the sinful nation will be led into captivity (9:9,10).

    When Jesus confronts the same mindset about keeping records of good and bad behaviors, he warns:

> Woe to you...hypocrites! for you tithe mint and dill and cummin, and have neglected the weightier matters of the law, justice and mercy and faith. (Matt. 23:23)

    On a previous occasion, Jesus answers Peter's question about forgiving a brother. "Shall it be seven times?" Jesus responds, "I do not say to you seven times, but seventy times seven" (Matt. 18:22).

Meditation: O Divine Reckoning One, Your tally sheet is totally different than my own. Your awesome mercy changes all scores.

Exodus 34:9   Isaiah 55:7   Jeremiah 31:34   Matthew 6:12,14   Mark 2:7   Ephesians 1:7

99 Beautiful Names of God

83   The Compassionate   ٱلرَّؤُوفُ AR-RA'UF

The Lord is merciful and gracious. Psalm 103:8

Ar-Ra'uf draws together all of the divine names expressing mercy and compassion (cf number 82) and compels God's creatures to look at God himself with eyes of pity and compassion. There is the traditional Arab saying, "My mercy overcomes my wrath." God shows us might, power, and glory, and we can be overcome by them; yet the Lord wants us also to be overcome by his divine expression of his compassionate love.

Any Hebrew root for this word, Ar-Ra'uf, will have to depend on further understanding of a similar Bible word meaning trickle or flow. Psalm 65 pictures the tracks of a heavenly chariot that drips with fatness, and "the pastures of the wilderness drip" (11,12). Another rare use of the term presents a natural event, a rain shower, combined with a message about salvation:

> Let the skies rain down righteousness; let the earth open, that salvation may
> sprout forth, and let it cause righteousness to spring up also. (Isa. 45:8)

The modern Arabic term for nosebleed is based upon this ancient Canaanite[1] word which has a minor but significant variation in the middle consonant for the name for God.

The subject of God's pity for his people extends throughout the Scriptures. The most widely used terms are built upon *rahum* (numbers 1 and 2) but there are other words that reveal this attribute, such as the profound thoughts conveyed in the Book of Lamentations. Within this volume, the weeping prophet Jeremiah speaks for the ruined city of Jerusalem. The prophet pleads with those who are passing by:

> Look and see if there is any sorrow like my sorrow which was brought upon
> me, which the Lord inflicted on me on the day of his fierce anger. (Lam. 1:12)

Judgment, not mercy, seems to be the theme of this short, sorrowful book—"The Lord has destroyed without mercy" (2:2). The prophet himself breaks down, "My eyes will flow without ceasing, without respite" (3:49). Jesus, the Anointed One, also within the environs of Jerusalem, duplicates the remorse of the prophet Jeremiah:

> "O Jerusalem, Jerusalem, killing the prophets and stoning those who are sent
> to you! How often would I have gathered your children together as a hen
> gathers her brood under her and you would not!" (Matt. 23:37)

Within hours he is praying alone in the Garden of Gethsemane. The agonizing prayer is accompanied by Jesus' "sweat like great drops of blood falling on the ground" (Luke 22:44). His prayer that the cup of the Father's chastisement be removed is not answered at the moment (Matt. 26:39) as he is led to the place of the skull to be crucified. While his blood flows from five fresh wounds, he cries out for mercy: "My God, my God, why hast thou forsaken me?" (Matt. 27:46). The scenes of the cross are not pleasant, and they evoke defiance and denials, but the images also call for human empathy toward God's great message of salvation and forgiveness.

Meditation: Please accept my highest praises for Your grace that flows from the cross of Calvary.

Deuteronomy 19:13   Psalm 116:5   Isaiah 63:9   Matthew 18:33   1 Peter 3:8   James 5:11

---

[1] Dahood, vol. 2, p. 116.

99 Beautiful Names of God

84 King Over All Earthly Kingdoms   مَـالِكُ الْمُلْكُ   MALIK-UL-MULK

All of the kings of the earth shall praise you, O, Lord. Psalm 138:4

The first half of this two-part name for God, Al-Malik, has been introduced in name number 3. The second half of this name provides an appreciation of the richness of this word in Arabic which first signifies owner, possession and property, and secondly a king. The Hebrew term is almost exclusively limited to king and other members of royalty. The title for Jesus as King of kings, in the Arabic and English versions of the Bible, is a worthy translation of the Greek.

God, as the Sovereign Lord over all material things as well as over all other kingdoms, places a designated name for God alongside those things and persons which are not part of the unity of God. This combination of God's name with his creatures is part of a Bible pattern that begins with the king-priest who meets Abraham in the Valley of the Kings. Melchizedek, king of righteousness, is also king of Salem (Peace), according to Genesis 14:17. Jesus' priestly line is traced to this ancient king (Heb. 5:5,6).

When Jesus assumes the title Son of Man, he showed his respect for the spiritual and non-spiritual aspects of both "Son" and "Man." The uniqueness of Jesus' birth, his ministry of healing and raising the dead, and his own resurrection adequately qualifies Jesus, the Messiah, to be both a divinely-appointed Son and one who is acquainted with humankind. Jesus feels the pain of his death and separation from his heavenly Father (Matt. 26:39, 27:46). He speaks about the Son of Man having no place to lay his head (Luke 9:58), and says that he will appear "seated at the right hand of the power of God" (22:69).

The prophet Isaiah spells out some of the human names of the coming One that are fulfilled by Jesus Christ. He will be a "child," a "son," who will be given the reins of government and called by these names—"Wonderful Counselor, Mighty God, Everlasting Father, Prince of Peace" (Isa. 9:6). The names provide both a divine and a human face to a person "who will rule upon the throne of David and over his kingdom to establish it...with justice and with righteousness from this time forth and for evermore" (9:7).

"King of kings" is a name that identifies Jesus in Paul's letter to Timothy along with "Lord of lords" (1 Tim. 6:15). These honored titles are placed in the closing section of the letter where he recalls Jesus' trial before Pontius Pilate (6:13). It was this Roman official who insisted upon placing the title on the cross, "Jesus of Nazareth, the King of the Jews." The sign named both the criminal, Jesus, and the crime of blasphemy for the onlookers in Jerusalem on that fateful day and forever (John 19:18f).

The Book of Revelation is filled with vivid portrayals of events that will take place in the future, including a battle that will be won by the Lamb who is called "Lord of lords and King of kings" (Rev. 17:14). Those servants of God who survive with the Lamb will be hailed as "chosen and faithful" (17:14).

Meditation: O Majestic Lord, Your possession of my life is perfect, lacking nothing in this world or the next.

Psalm 72:1   Isaiah 32:1   Zephaniah 3:14f   Luke 12:8   John 19:14   2 Corinthians 6:10

99 Beautiful Names of God

85 Possessor of Sublimity and Generosity — DHŪL-JALĀL-WAL-IKRĀM

O Lord, our Lord, how majestic is your name in all the earth! Psalm 8:1

This beautiful name of God consolidates two names that were presented previously (41, the Sublime, and 42, the Bountiful One) with minor internal changes in pronunciations from the earlier listing. These two names have an attractive sound, making them both names of individuals and the names of places of natural beauty, such as the Sea of Galilee and Mount Carmel. In their present form, the names Jalal and Ikram take on a more regal air when they are used in direct address to kings and other high officials, much like the English, "Your esteemed majesty."

Dhul is a unique Arabic word that is used here to tie together two attributes and is found in the Qur'an as a nickname.[1] The prophet Jonah is called *"dhul-Nun,"* the possessor of the fish (Sura 21:87). Alexander the Great, *"dhul-Qarnayn,"* the possessor of two horns (18:85), is based upon Daniel's vision of the ram with the two horns (Dan. 8:1f).

Both of these names for God suggest a buoyant force that can be felt through human senses. Words derived from *jalil* reveal pleasant sounds, like gentle waves of the sea (Ps. 42:7), and well-rounded objects such as bowls (1 Kings 7:41). Isaiah's description of the heavens rolling like a scroll (34:4) impact the listener with powerful auditory and visual images. The many words stemming from the second part of this name, *karim*, open up further vistas of bountiful vineyards, referred to in Amos 5:11. Both of these words have gloomy connotations in the Hebrew Bible where jalil is associated with a heap of stones or a ruin (Jer. 9:10), and karim, the vineyards, are often trampled by invading armies or eaten by locusts (Jer. 12:10).

The coming together of bowls, waving sea, unrolling scrolls, pleasant accolades of praises, amidst desolation and destruction is evident in the Book of Revelation. This last book in the Christian canon is written by John the apostle to reveal to his fellow servants, Jesus Christ as the Savior of the world, and events that would take place in the future (1:1). John is lifted up to heaven, and while he is in the Spirit (4:2), he witnesses scores of scenes of beautiful, sublime and terrifying events yet to be unfolded in coming generations.

Many of the images are residual images of temple utensils, like golden bowls (5:8); but most are inspired by the opening of seven scrolls, accompanied by grander and even more majestic visions and sounds. Animals and natural events, like thunder, earthquakes, and storms, are featured with the opening of the first seals of the scrolls (6:1f). Following the fourth seal, wars, pestilence, and the "wrath of the Lamb" (6:16) fall upon the people. Throughout the visions, the voices of the magnificent international choir cry out, "Salvation belongs to our God who sits upon the throne, and to the Lamb" (7:10). The awesome God will remain in the midst of the people to wipe away all tears (7:17).

Meditation: My voice is subject to many whims of temperament and disturbing social winds, but help me sing Your praises at all times, O Majestic and Bountiful One.

Psalm 111:3   Proverbs 28:10   Philippians 4:8,9,17   Revelation 8:1-5

---

[1] Schimmel, p. 66

99 Beautiful Names of God

86 The Equitable AL-MUQSIT

Of a truth, your God is God of gods and Lord of kings, and a revealer of mysteries. Daniel 2:47

Al-Muqsit had its origin during the time when the Aramaic language was dominant in the Middle East, which was roughly equivalent to the period of the Persian empire (500 B.C. to A.D. 250). This name for God is not found in the Qur'an; and, with Al-'Adl, the Just One (number 29), this name shares many of the same definitions of justice, righteousness, and truth.

Just and equitable weights were a concern for the people of God, which is apparent in several of the Hebrew words that predate the spread of the Aramaic language. "A false balance is an abomination to the Lord," states Proverbs 11:1, "but a just weight is his delight." The term for weight is a designation for an ordinary stone or pebble. "Shekel" introduces a standard weight, and gradually silver coins with that name replace the stones. That does not stop the use and manipulation of "unjust weights." The prophet Amos denounced those who "trample upon the needy" by falsifying the money standard to their own wicked advantage. They boasted

> ...that we may make the ephah small and the shekel great, and deal deceitfully with false balances; that we may buy the poor for silver and the needy for a pair of sandals. (Amos 8:5,6)

"A just balance and scale are the Lord's," says Proverbs 16:11. Another proverb warns against injustices when the poor are robbed by those who "knew what was right and true" (22:22). In the prophecy of Daniel, it is the polytheistic monarch Nebuchadnezzar who recognizes the truth of Daniel's God as the God of all gods (2:47). At the time of the mysterious handwritten message on the wall, Daniel delivers the interpretation of Mene, Mene, Tekel, Parsin—the Chaldean kingdom had been "weighed in the balances and found wanting" (5:25f).

Social and economic injustices are aggravated by the fact that there is little legal recourse for the poor of the land throughout biblical times. Jesus directs his would-be disciples to share equitably with those who have less. Anyone who has two coats or extra food, "let him share with those who have none" (Luke 3:11). He instructs tax collectors and soldiers not to rob "by violent or by false accusation" (3:12,14).

Jesus' own trial is a mockery, even to the justice system available at that time, as is recognized by one of the criminals who dies on a cross on that momentous Good Friday in Jerusalem. Instead of railing out at those who are applying the full measure of capital punishment, this unnamed thief rebukes another criminal for cursing God and his tormentors. "Do you not fear God, since you are under the same" death sentence? He continues, "We indeed are justly condemned and we are receiving the due reward. But this man has done nothing wrong" (Luke 23:40f). What follows is the strongest statement ever made about God's unique distribution of justice and unmerited grace. Jesus answers the request of the dying thief, "Truly, I say to you, today you will be with me in Paradise" (23:43).

Meditation: The weight of my guilt is heavy, but You control the scale, O Lord, my blessed Redeemer.

Deuteronomy 25:13,15 Psalm 45:6 Proverbs 27:3 Matthew 23:23 Philippians 4:8

87 The Gatherer   اَلْجَامِعُ AL-JAME'

Thus says the Lord God, who gathers the outcasts of Israel, "I will gather yet others to him besides those already gathered." Isaiah 56:8

Whether one is referring to a university, a sociology class, a stamp collection, a group of any size, the basic word for gathering is ubiquitous in areas of the world where Arabic is a dominant language. Since Friday is the designated prayer day at the mosque, both "Friday" (*yaum aljuma'*) and "mosque" (*jaami'*) are words that are formed from the same consonants that make up this name for God, Al-Jame'. The word does not appear in this form in the original Bible languages, but there are numerous Hebrew words that speak of the tribes of Israel gathering themselves together for both peaceful and military purposes (Gen. 34:30, 49:2).

Along with gathering and assembling armies and people, there are more utilitarian gatherings of grapes (Deut. 24:21), temple vessels (2 Chron. 28:24) and stones (Eccl. 3:5). As the prophets prepare the nation for the time they will spend in exile, these same men of God announced that there would be a future gathering in their land. Long before the threat of the Babylonian invasion and the return under Persian rule, Micah presents God's promise of the gathering:

> I will surely gather all of you, O Jacob, I will gather the remnant of Israel; I will set them together in a fold, like a flock in its pasture. (2:12)

Jeremiah witnesses the dispersing of the people from the city of Jerusalem, but offers consolation on behalf of a returning remnant. "I will gather the remnant of my flock out of all the countries...and I will bring them back to their fold" (23:3). After the return of the Jews to Jerusalem, in the middle of the fifth century, Ezra thanks the Just, the Equitable One, for gathering the remnant together (Ezra 9:15).

The Aramaic word for gathering of the king's counselors at the dedication of the idol (Dan. 2:2,27) names two outstanding institutions in the Middle East today. The word for the parliament in Israel is *Knesset* and the word for church in Arabic is *kanesa*. It is very likely that Jesus used the latter term as he spoke a dialect of the Aramaic language and visited often in synagogues which were also called kanesa.

Jesus Christ opens his public ministry in his hometown of Nazareth where he is invited to preach in the synagogue. There on the Sabbath day he selects a text from Isaiah, "to proclaim the acceptable year of the Lord" (Luke 4:16f). His meetings in other synagogues are often closely observed by the temple legalists who confront him on such issues as not washing properly and healing on the Sabbath (Luke 6:6).

Saul, when he is a persecutor, has orders to destroy the believers in the Way of Jesus Christ in the Damascus synagogues (Acts 9:2), but after a confrontation with the risen Lord he enters the same synagogues to bring the glad tidings of Jesus, "the Son of God" (9:20). Paul the apostle continues his proclamation of Jesus, the Head of the Church (Greek: called out gathering). He writes to the Ephesians that God gave Jesus a name "above every name" and "made him the head over all things for the church" (1:22).

Meditation: You have been a Generous One to gather all people, nations, and tribes to Your eternal kingdom.

Exodus 35:1   1 Samuel 7:5   Psalm 147:2   Matthew 18:20   John 4:36   Ephesians 5:25

88 The Self Sufficient, The Rich One  AL-GHANĪ

You visit the earth and water it, you greatly enrich it. Psalm 65:9

Abraham had many cattle (Gen. 13:2) which helps illustrate this name and the following name (number 89, the Enricher) in the Hebrew Bible. The grasslands on the plains and on the gentle slopes of Palestine sustained the herds during biblical times which remind the psalmist of God's great riches. Along with every beast of the forest, God owns "the cattle on a thousand hills" (50:10). Another psalm praised the Lord for his multiple acts of creation, including land and sea creatures (Ps. 104:24,25).

In Proverbs many verses speak about riches that refer to the bountiful God's claim for himself; for example, "Riches and honor are with me, enduring wealth and prosperity" (8:18). Several proverbs in chapter 22 instruct the listener that "the fear of the Lord is riches and honor and life" (v. 4). "A good name is to be chosen rather than great riches" opens this chapter; and rich and poor are classless in verse 2. "The rich and the poor meet together; the Lord is the maker of them all." The middle way is the most suitable, according to the author of the following proverb:

> Give me neither poverty nor riches; feed me with the food that is most needful for me, lest I be full, and deny you, and say, "Who is the Lord?" or lest I be poor, and steal, and profane the name of my God. (30:8,9)

Amos starts his life in eighth-century Israel as a simple farmer who sees the rich exploiting the poor of the land. He lashes out at the conspicuous wealth of the urban classes as they "oppress the poor, and crush the needy," and at the women he hurls this accusation: "You say to your husbands, 'Bring that we may drink!'" (4:1). When the nation lies under siege at the time of Jeremiah, the prophet of God compares the desolation of Jerusalem to a fallen woman. "What do you mean that you dress yourself in scarlet," he mocked, "that you deck yourself with ornaments of gold?" (Jer. 4:30).

Gold and silver does not impress the Lord God when he gives Jeremiah an idea of his standards for wealth:

> Let not the wise man glory in his wisdom...let not the rich man glory in his riches; but let him who glories, glory in this, that he understands and knows me, that I am the Lord, who practice steadfast love, justice, and righteousness in the earth. (Jer. 9:23)

The words Jesus Christ selects are from many prophets, but when he initiates his ministry in Nazareth he turns to Isaiah, where he reads: "The Spirit of the Lord is upon me, because he has anointed me to preach the gospel to the poor" (Luke 4:18). At his concluding talk with his faithful few, Jesus cautions them not to look for him beyond the "stranger," "naked one," "hungry one," and the "thirsty" ones (Matt. 25:31f). A modern-day holy one, Mother Theresa of Calcutta stated that she met Jesus every day "in the needy, suffering souls she saw and tended."[1]

Meditation: Lord, gentle Lord and Master, the carnal life seeks out riches and raiment, but You offer my spirit so much more.

Genesis 31:16   Job 36:19   Proverbs 28:2   Matthew 13:22   Romans 11:12,33

---

[1] Malcolm Muggeridge, *Something Beautiful for God* (New York: Ballantine Books, 1973), p. 130.

89 The Enricher  AL-MUGHNĪ

To them God chose to make known how great among the Gentiles are the riches of the glory of this mystery. Colossians 1:27

Riches in the Hebrew Bible are based upon cattle and grazing lands, as this name and the previous name for God indicate. The term "rich" moves to a more metaphysical word in the closing books of the Hebrew Bible, and it reaches its spiritual zenith with the teaching of Jesus and Paul in the New Covenant era. Jesus speaks in the parable of the sower about the "deceitfulness of riches" (Matt. 13:22), but he also compares the kingdom of heaven to a treasure hid in a field that is later purchased at a great cost (13:44). God, as the enriching, empowering sovereign, is best identified by Jesus' words, "Seek first his kingdom and his righteousness, and all of these things shall be yours as well" (6:33).

God, Al-Mughni, is the one who is enlarging and expanding his possessions, much like the early patriarchs who increased their land to support their cattle (Gen. 13:6). The latter sections of Isaiah are filled with references to Gentiles, the non-Israelite nations, which were also considered a rich area for expansion. Some of the prophecies are repeated in strictly earthly statements that are to vindicate the coming defeat of the city of Jerusalem and Judah's captivity in Babylonia (Isa. 62:2); but many other promises refer to the Gentiles, the nations, in much more hopeful words. "And nations shall come to your light" (60:3) and messengers "shall declare my glory among the nations" (66:19).

The apostle Paul becomes the faithful witness to the nations of the Gentiles; and he promotes his office as an apostle, based upon his unique calling. Writing to a largely non-Jewish flock in the great metropolis of Ephesus late in his life, Paul sets forth how he has been enriched by God in Christ and then develops a theme of the wonderful inheritance that all believers have in this once hidden, mysterious faith. He thanks his God for his salvation and builds on that foundation:

> In [Christ] we have redemption through his blood, the forgiveness of our trespasses, according to the riches of his grace which he lavished upon us. (Eph. 1:7,8)

He finds the treasure in the field that Jesus speaks about in the parable, as the gift of the Holy Spirit, "the guarantee of our inheritance" waiting for our full "possession of it" (Eph. 1:14). Paul realizes there is more invested in us in the "coming ages" when we are going to be shown the "immeasurable riches of his grace" (2:7); but his greatest joy is expressed when he sees the nations, those outside of the "commonwealth of Israel" (2:12), come to God through Jesus, the Messiah.

> So you are no longer strangers and sojourners, but you are fellow citizens with the saints and members of the household of God. (2:19)

He calls these Gentiles "fellow heirs" and "partakers" of the gospel, which is so dear to his own calling as a minister of the gospel (3:6,7). "To me, though I am the very least of all the saints, this grace was given, to preach to the Gentiles the unsearchable riches of Christ...[which was] hidden for ages...[but] now...made known..." (3:8-10).

Meditation: I treasure the thoughts of Your unspeakable riches yet to be shared with me in glory, O Enricher of my soul.

Deuteronomy 28:12 Isaiah 61:6,9 Malachi 1:11 Matthew 6:19 Ephesians 3:16

99 Beautiful Names of God

90 The Preventer, The Delayer  AL-MĀNI'

For the Lord God is a sun and shield; he bestows favor and honor. No good thing does the Lord withhold from those who walk uprightly. Psalm 84:11

The Hebrew Bible uses this word regularly as an ordinary expression for withholding an item from someone. The Greek of the New Testament has both a practical use as well as a definite theological use in describing a "restraining force" that is found in Paul's writing. The word has wide usage in modern Arabic, but it is not found in the Qur'an as a name for God.

Paul's second Thessalonian letter has a short reference to the restraining one who is presently active in the spiritual world. Paul asks that his readers ponder what he has shared with them in his earlier personal contacts with them (1 Thess. 2:5f).

> And you know what is restraining him [the man of lawlessness] now so that he may be revealed in his time. For the mystery of lawlessness is already at work; only he who now restrains it will do so until he is out of the way. (2 Thess. 2:6,7)

There are several interpretations of what this "restraining person/power" could be that range all the way from the imperial Roman empire to modern missionary activity.[1] The name Al-Mani' suggests that God is the One who restrains evil as well.

One day when Jesus confronts the demonic forces, many of these demons cried out, "You are the Son of God," but Jesus prevents, i.e. rebukes, them because "they knew that he was the Messiah" (Luke 4:41). This happens early in his ministry when he does not want the Messianic mystery to be revealed. Some time later, Jesus heals a blind man who is encouraged to openly confess his healing and hold back nothing, even when he and his parents are threatened (John 9:24f).

The Lord, as the Hinderer, held back many rivers (Ezek. 31:15), rain (Amos 4:7) and light from the wicked (Job 38:15). The Hebrew uses the same word sources as Al-Mani' to declare all of the wonderful things that were not held back from the hand of God. Nehemiah records the words of the priest Ezra, reviewing the glorious care that God provides for the faithful people during the forty years in the Sinai wilderness.

> You gave your good Spirit to instruct them, and did not withhold your manna from their mouth and gave them water for their thirst. (9:20)

King David glorifies God for not holding back when he addresses the Mighty One, "You have not withheld the request of [the king's] lips" (Ps. 21:2).

On a couple occasions, the Lord prevents a couple from having a child but that is later compensated by the birth of Isaac to Abraham and Sarah (Gen. 16:2) and the birth of Joseph to Rachel and Jacob (Gen. 30:2,24).

Meditation: Wherever You guide me, there are warning signs to stay on the right track, O Watcher of my destiny.

Numbers 14:11   1 Samuel 25:26   Romans 1:18   1 Corinthians 11:2   1 Thessalonians 5:21

---

[1] William F. Arndt and Wilbur Gingrich, *A Greek-English Lexicon of the New Testament and Other Early Christian Literature* (Chicago: University of Chicago Press, 1952), p. 423.

91 The Distresser, The Destroyer  AD-ḌĀRR

Then the anger of the Lord was kindled against his people. Psalm 106:40

The idea that the God of love and peace can direct his anger against his own people has been difficult to accept for all people of faith. For the declared enemies of God, there is the expectation that God's anger will be revealed against them; but it is not expected to fall on those whose heritage gives at least a token offering to God, who is the One demanding and receiving full respect in former days.

This name doubles with the next name, the Favorer, to show for the last time in this list of 99 names the spectrum of God's interactions with his people. The Hebrew root word closest to this name, Ad-Darr, refers to hostility and defrauding. The word does appear in the Qur'an (10:107) and it is inferred in several suras that mention the "people of Noah" who were destroyed by the flood (Suras 9:70 and 22:42).

The biblical narrative reporting the destruction of the earth by the flood reveals both the severity and the mercy of God. He severely judges his creatures who drowned in the flood, but Noah is declared a righteous man, "blameless in his generation; Noah walked with God" (Gen. 6:9). God tells Noah that he plans to "make an end of all flesh" but at the same time he provides Noah with instructions on how to build an ark that would preserve life on the earth (6:13,14). "We saved him and those with him in the fully-laden ark" (Sura 26:118).

God reminds the Israelites of his power when he saves the tribes from the vanquished Egyptian army at the Red Sea crossing. God recalls for them several occurrences in which he destroys some of the very people whom he was trying to save (Deut. 11:5,6). Toward the end of the period of the conquest, Joshua gives warning about serving other gods that would lead a jealous God to turn upon the people and consume them (Josh. 24:20).

The severest test for the people comes when they are reduced to a fraction of their former number, humiliated in defeat and carried off to bondage in Babylonia. It is the prophet Jeremiah who writes about this action caused by God:

> You have rejected me, says the Lord, you keep going backward; so I have stretched out my hand against you and destroyed you;—I am weary of relenting. (15:6)

The song of death and destruction is not the final word, however. The promise of restoration is always there:

> I will deliver you out of the hand of the wicked, and redeem you from the grasp of the ruthless. (15:21)

The cycles of sin–judgment–restoration are obvious throughout the Hebrew Bible. They are personified in the ministry of Jesus when he is "reckoned with the sinners" to fulfill the Scriptures (Luke 22:37). Isaiah provides the scriptural background, not only for Christ's judgment but also for his restoration. "In his humiliation justice was denied him...for his life is taken up from the earth" (Isa. 53:7,12; Acts 8:33).

Meditation: O my righteous Savior, save me from sins when Your holiness is offended by my unholy thoughts and actions.

Exodus 23:22 Ruth 1:21 Psalm 44:2,3 Matthew 10:28 Luke 19:47 Revelation 11:18

99 Beautiful Names of God

92 The Propitious, The One Who Grants Favor  AN-NĀFI'

But Noah found favor in the eyes of the Lord. Genesis 6:8

Noah's full life of 950 years shows that he did his best to preserve his small family from the surrounding wickedness. However, because of an unguarded moment in his life when one of his sons caught a glimpse of his father's nakedness, the family name went into decline (Gen. 9:20f). This spectrum of human weakness and divine favor is worthy of note when we see these two names of God in close proximity. While men and women experience a range of divine destruction and divine blessing at different moments in time, God's mysterious unity places all of these names in one moment, one eternity of time.

The name An-Nafi' serves as a helpful word in translating the Semitic term "found favor in the eyes of" throughout the Bible, where the word *nafi'* is not found. Among the prophets who find favor, or grace, in God's eyes are Noah (Gen. 6:8), Abraham (Gen. 18:3), and Joseph (Acts 7:10). Joseph not only wins God's favor but is promoted into Pharaoh's court because of God's unswerving attention. God promises Moses that the Hebrews living in Egypt will also find favor among the Egyptians (Ex. 3:21). David composes psalms that praise the Lord for "all his benefits" (103:2). The martyr Stephen, while preaching his final sermon in Jerusalem, mentions "David, who found favor in the sight of God" (Acts 7:46).

We know little about Jesus' childhood aside from the birth narratives and his one visit with Mary and Joseph to the temple (Luke 2:41f). This description of the youth and the young adult fill in some of the silence of those years: "Jesus increased in wisdom and in stature, and in favor with God and man" (2:52). God's favors on his servants certainly do not go unnoticed by those who come into contact with these benefactors of God's grace. Ruth the Moabitess receives the full attention of Boaz (Ruth 2:13), and Esther attracts the eyes of the king of all Persians by her queenly demeanor in his court (Est. 5:2).

In the early days of the church in Jerusalem, the new followers of the Way of Jesus also "found favor with all of the people" (Acts 2:47). Later, following Stephen's death and the persecution of the believers, they take on some practical matters that benefit the dispersed groups of Christians. There was the collection of money that Paul dealt with to benefit the impoverished churches in Jerusalem (1 Cor. 16:1f). He sees the advancement of his mission endeavors as a mutual benefit to himself and the areas he selects to visit (2 Cor. 1:15,16). Paul admonished his fellow servants to "apply themselves to good deeds; these are excellent and profitable to men" (Titus 3:8). Even to slaves who serve believing masters, he offered this advice: to attend their work with honor and respect "so that the name of God and the teaching may not be defamed" (1 Tim. 6:1).

Meditation: Your favor to me is sublime, O Gracious One. Let Your likeness be seen by all who observe my works.

Genesis 39:21 Numbers 11:11 Psalm 116:12 Daniel 1:4 Luke 1:28,30 Acts 7:10

93 The Light  AN-NŪR

The Lord will be an everlasting light. Isaiah 60:19

Orient, the source of the light, is one of many words that passed through Mediterranean waters to European languages with only minor changes from its Hebrew and Arabic origins. Persian carpet weavers, poets and architects all found the rich imagery of Sura 24 a compelling source of various art forms. The sura was named An-Nur after these words:

> God is Light of the heavens and the earth. The likeness of Light is to a niche containing a lamp enclosed in glass like a radiant star...God guides to the Light whom he wills. (Sura 24:35)

From the beginning to the end of Scripture, the brilliance of sun and moon, light and life have been contrasted with dark, shadows, the Pit of Sheol, and death. Humankind must see these as opposites, but they all belong to God's mysterious universe that begins the first day of creation with the creation of light which is separated from darkness (Gen. 1:3). Abraham sees a flaming torch in the dark of the night when God assures him of the promise that his descendants would live in the land of Canaan (Gen. 15:17). Abraham leaves the land of Ur (the Light) to follow God's promise that his descendants will be numberless like the starry heavens (15:5,7).

An angel of the Lord appears to Moses in a burning bush and God directs him to put off his shoes for he stands on holy ground (Ex. 3:2f). Just before the dramatic miracle of the Red Sea crossing, God provides the "pillar of cloud by day and the pillar of fire by night" (Ex. 13:22). At the giving of the law of God to Moses on Mount Sinai, the mountains shake and lightning flashes from the sky (20:18). The symbols of God's continual presence are incorporated into the worship services of the tent meeting in the wilderness and later in the temple of Solomon (Lev. 24:1f and 1 Kings 7:48). The lamps did not burn continually as the dark days of war and famine and captivity overpowered the kingdom of Judah. Jeremiah prophesies the lowering of lights:

> Give glory to the Lord your God before he brings darkness; before your feet stumble on the twilight mountains, and while you look for light he turns it into gloom and makes it deep darkness. (Jer. 13:16)

Earlier, the prophet Amos tells the people of the northern kingdom of Israel that the expected day of the Lord is a day of "darkness and not light, and gloom with no brightness in it" (5:20).

The metaphor of light and darkness is used by Jesus when he warns the people that they must be prepared to meet the bridal party at any time. He tells the story of ten maidens selected for a wedding, but only half of them have oil to light their festive lamps to greet the bridegroom (Matt. 25:1f). In one of his great "I am's" of John's gospel, Jesus announces, "I am the light of the world; he who follows me will not walk in darkness" (John 8:12). The final city of the living God will be where the temple is permanently replaced by the Almighty and where there will be no "need of sun or moon to shine upon it, for the glory of God is its light, and its lamp is the Lamb" (Rev. 21:23).

Meditation: Gracious God, You have condescended to be with me at my lowest points. I pray that You will keep me in Your light.

Judges 7:6 Psalm 119:30 Isaiah 42:6,16 Matthew 4:16 John 1:4-9 Ephesians 5:8-14

94 The Guide  AL-HĀDĪ

When the Spirit of truth comes, he will guide you into all truth. John 16:13

This name for God is loaded with meanings for all three of the faiths emerging from Abraham's faithfulness. There are several other words, prior to Daniel, that refer to counselors and guides; but the Persian envoys are called *haddaberim* in Daniel 3:24. The word is shortened and its meaning broadened by New Testament Greek times, when it served as a word for either a road, a code of conduct, or a whole way of life. The Greek word *hodos* suggests an association with the Arabic Al-Hadi.

Jesus employs this word when he speaks to his disciples in John 14:6. "I am the way." Up to this time, John records these sayings of Jesus: "I am the Bread of Life," Ar-Razzaq, name number 17 (6:48); "I am the Light," An-Nur, name 93 (8:12); "I am the Door, Opening to the sheep," Al-Fattah, name 18 (10:7); "I am the good Shepherd," Al-Muqit, name 39 (10:11); "I am the Resurrection and the Life," Al-Ba'ith, name 49; Al-Qayyum, name 63 and name 62, Al-Hayy (11:25). The three I am's of John 14:6 include the names, the Truth, Al-Haqq, number 51, and the Life, Al-Hayy, number 62. The names that Jesus calls himself, covering daily bread to eternal salvation and life everlasting, reveal the all-sufficient One's unique grace where he was bold to add, "No one comes to the Father, but by me" (John 14:6).

For Muslims, eternal guidance is based upon the way of the law which is a combination of the former pre-Islamic laws, the Torah of Moses, the Qur'an, and the sayings and practices of Muhammad. The former scriptures are worthy guides, according to Sura 3:2: "He has revealed the Torah and the Gospel for the guidance of men." No one can be sure of the precise number of laws that have to be followed, and anyone who desires to be part of the *"ulama"* (the knowers) will keep whole libraries of legal opinions close at hand. According to Islamic law, every human action must fit into one of five categories that range from acceptable to forbidden behavior.[1]

Believers in Jesus Christ throughout all ages have been provided a personal model of behavior, which means there is a dynamic personal dimension to following the Way of Jesus. Also, there is the gift of the Holy Spirit who is the guide, in the place of Christ (John 16:13). Secondly, the teaching of the apostles about Jesus in the Book of Acts is an important step in keeping the gospel as a body of truth. Even the message of the Holy Spirit was a hotly-debated topic for the followers of the Way among Corinthian believers (Acts 19:9). Wherever the apostles ventured there were disputes and setbacks; but in the midst of his own trial in Jerusalem, Paul testifies of the Way:

> But this I admit to you, that according to the Way, which they call a sect, I worship the God of our fathers, believing everything laid down by the law...there will be a resurrection of the just and the unjust. (Acts 24:14f)

Meditation: Guide me in the straight path, the way that Jesus my Lord took to follow the will of his heavenly Father.

Isaiah 40:13   Proverbs 12:20   Daniel 3:27   Luke 1:79   Romans 11:33   Revelation 15:3

---

[1] Glasse, p. 362

95   The Incomparable, The Purpose Setter    AL-BADĪ'

We know that in everything God works for good to those who love him, who are called according to his purpose. Romans 8:28

The name Al-Badi' comes from the same Hebrew root as the name listed as Al-Mubdi, number 58, where there are only a few biblical references to the deceitful devices of humans. A couple of verses reveal David's plea to God to thwart evil planning:

> Let them be put to shame and dishonor who seek after my life! Let them be turned back and confounded who devise evil against me! (Ps. 35:4)

The enemies of King David cannot be trusted, "For they do not seek peace" and "they conceive words of deceit" (v. 20).

There is another name for God that is not found in Al-Ghazali's list of divine names. This name appears in Sura 3, where Jesus is facing plots by his enemies to kill him. The Qur'an responds by stating that "God is the best of all plotters" (3:54). There are many cunning plans to defeat the plans of God in the Bible, but none deserves the attention suggested by this name. Al-Badi', God the Originator of heaven and earth, is also identified as the One who wills a thing, says "Be" and it is (Sura 2:117).

The most helpful terms to understand God's plans and purposes are found in the writings of Paul where he engages his opponents by appeals to reason rather than to some deterministic view of revelation. The apostle does use the word "purpose" to show that God does project for the future what he has originated in his timeless eternity, but there is plenty of room for human responses. In the delicate subject of electing some to greater glory than others, Paul refers to the two sons of Isaac, who before they were born were "elected" to fulfill a call to a definite service, "in order that God's purpose of election might continue, not because of works but because of his call" (Rom. 9:11).

Throughout his other writings, Paul is even more clear that the predestined ones are those who "have been destined and appointed to live for the praise of his glory" (Eph. 1:12). The "eternal purposes" are described in this same epistle and are "realized in Christ Jesus" (3:11). Paul is not convinced that God has worked out every moment of a person's life, sending one to paradise and another to hell. The purposes of God are stated in general terms, linking salvation and enduring hardships, that "conform to the image of God's Son" (Rom. 8:29). Paul expresses his life mission to his young protégé, Timothy, in his prison letter:

> Now you have observed my teaching, my conduct, my aim in life, my faith, my patience, my love, my steadfastness, my persecutions, my sufferings, what befell me at Antioch, at Iconium, and at Lystra, what persecutions I endured; yet from them all the Lord rescued me. (2 Tim. 3:10,11)

Meditation: My magnificent Lord, You are forever originating good for Your world. Help me to seek Your purposes for improving Your new creation in Christ in me.

Job 17:11   Nehemiah 8:4   Jeremiah 49:20   Ephesians 4:11f   Philippians 2:1f

96   The Enduring, The Everlasting  AL-BĀQĪ

But you [God] are the same, and your years have no end. The children of your servants shall dwell secure; their posterity shall be established before you.
Psalm 102:27,28

Name number 68, As-Samad, refers to foundations and the establishment of the world in an eternal past time, while Al-Baqi has its root meanings of left over, the remaining, referring to time in the future, the Everlasting. Both concepts of eternity are derived from a human view of changing time, but God's view is that time does not change. This name, Al-Baqi, does not appear in the Hebrew Scriptures, but the thoughts of eternity are apparent throughout all of the Bible. The author of Ecclesiastes ponders what God has communicated to him and what is still far from human comprehension:

> He has made everything beautiful in its time; also he has put eternity into man's mind, yet so that he cannot find what God has done from the beginning to the end. (3:11)

Human life has always concerned itself with the hereafter and what in this life will be part of some future existence. Powerful pharaohs constructed pyramids along the banks of the Nile where their slaves died and were buried next to their god-king. For the singers of the psalms the enduring things are the "fear of the Lord" (Ps. 19:9), David's seed (89:36), God's "righteousness" (111:3), and "his praise" (111:10).

One of the phrases on the lips of Jesus is, "he who endures to the end will be saved," which is recorded twice by Matthew. In the first instance, Jesus commissions the twelve disciples and tells them to visit "only the lost sheep of the house of Israel" (Matt. 10:5); but he does not end there, as he warns them that they will be "dragged before governors and kings for my sake, to bear witness before them and the Gentiles" (10:18). While the disciples are in custody, they are to speak, but it is the Holy Spirit who will speak through them (20). The Matthew account then speaks of the betrayals by family members which climax in the caution, "You will be hated by all for my name's sake," coupled with the promise, "But he who endures to the end will be saved" (22).

The Gospel of Mark corroborates the Matthew report of Jesus speaking to his disciples as they sit together on the Mount of Olives and look down on the Jerusalem temple. This time he speaks of those who will endure to the end in more apocalyptic terms, when again the enduring advocacy of the Holy Spirit will speak for the oppressed believers. In this setting he teaches about the things that will accompany the days of persecution, and lists a number of events that will be normative until the end of time. These include false prophets, wars, rumors of wars, earthquakes and famines (Mark 13:3f).

The single event that will indicate definite proof of the end of history is summed up by both Matthew and Mark:

> But he who endures to the end will be saved. And this gospel of the kingdom will be preached throughout the whole world as a testimony to all nations; and then the end will come. (Matt. 24:13,14).

Meditation: Grant me, O Eternal God, the courage to endure to the end of all things with joyful and hopeful spirit.

Exodus 18:23   Psalm 102:26   Mark 4:17   John 6:27   Hebrews 12:2,3,7

97 The Inheritor   ٱلْوَارِثُ AL-WĀRITH

The Lord God of Israel is their inheritance. Joshua 13:33

The Bible and the Qur'an agree that God is the Inheritor for which they share the same word; the full benefactor of his generous giving is God's creation. The texts of both documents speak about "inheriting the earth" (Ps. 37:11, Matt. 5:5 and Sura 19:40). The Bible passages say that the "meek shall inherit the earth," while the Qur'an, even though it could be referring to Jesus' words to his followers, states: "We shall inherit the earth and all who dwell upon it and unto us they shall return" (19:40).

Inheritances are troublesome for the people of God, as the distribution of land following the time of conquest painfully indicates. The biblical records understand that not all of the former people are dispossessed. The Canaanites remain in the land and some are forced into slavery (Josh. 16:10) while the Jebusites still control the city of Jerusalem, and David later has to purchase the threshing floor (1 Chron. 11:4,5; 21:18f); the tribes on the east Jordan bank are hardly a viable Israelite group, as the native Edomites (2 Chron. 21:8-10), Moabites (Ps. 60:8), and Gilead inhabitants (Judg. 10:8) are dominant throughout biblical times.

Many of these non-Israelites assimilate into the landscape, as noted by records showing the strength of the foreign gods and goddesses throughout the land of Israel and Judah (Jer. 1:16, 2 Chron. 28:25). Many other "strangers and foreigners" enter the land and are integrated into the society, as is the case with Uriah the Hittite (2 Sam. 11:3f). Ruth, the grandmother of King David, enters Israel from a pagan Moabite background and adopts fully the new faith (Ruth 1:15f).

Following the destructive battles and the exile of the nation of Judah, Jeremiah weeps over Jerusalem: "Our inheritance has been turned over to strangers, our homes to aliens" (Lam. 5:2). Many of these strangers become the poor of the land, a peasant, landless class during the times of war and famine. The Samaritans, a racially-mixed people, are further separated from the Jews as a disenfranchised religious group (John 4:4f).

Psalm 37 admonishes those who are suffering at the hands of evil men to "Trust in the Lord, and do good; so you will dwell in the land and enjoy security" (3). The psalm asks for the dispossessed to be patient and promises: "But the meek shall possess the land, and delight themselves in abundant prosperity" (11).

In Luke Jesus refers directly to these same poor of the land: "Blessed are you poor, for yours is the kingdom of heaven" (6:20), which is an expansion of words from the sermon recorded by Matthew: "Blessed are the meek, for they shall inherit the earth" (5:5). Jesus moves beyond that promise of lands and material prosperity when he speaks about the true eternal inheritance. The blessed ones he invites to "inherit the kingdom prepared for them from the foundation of the world" (Matt. 25:34).

Other New Covenant writers refer to these spiritual inheritances as the gift of the Holy Spirit (Eph. 1:13,14), Jesus as "the heir of all things" (Heb. 1:2), the gift of faith (Heb. 11:8) and heavenly glory for God's servants (1 Peter 1:4).

Meditation: Why do I concern myself with lesser things when You have provided me with such a great inheritance in Jesus Christ?

Genesis 28:4   Deuteronomy 4:20   Isaiah 66:22   Colossians 1:13   Revelation 21:7

99 Beautiful Names of God

98 The Right Guide 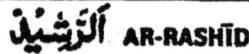 **AR-RASHĪD**

He guides the humble in what is right, and teaches the humble his way. Psalm 25:9

Any Hebrew origins of this Arabic name, Ar-Rashid, will be hard to prove, but images of the divinely guided path are apparent throughout the Bible. The first psalm presents the person who is blessed because he is in the way of the righteous (6) in contrast to the wicked ones who are condemned because they are not in "the congregation of the righteous" (5). The analogies of a tree, of ripening fruit, of a rushing stream, of a full year of leaves describe the person who neither walks, nor stands, nor sits in the way of sinners and scoffers. The person of rectitude has perpetual guidance: "But his delight is in the law of the Lord" (2).

While the well-counseled individual represents stability, the sinners are "like the chaff which the wind drives away" (4). They will not be able to "stand in the judgment" (5). The Qur'an grasps some of the similitudes of this opening psalm, where the good Word is compared to a "good tree which yields its fruit in its season" (Sura 14:24). The Word (*Kalimah*) is one of the Qur'anic names for the Messiah Jesus (3:39, 4:171); and in Sura 5, Jesus, son of Mary, comes, confirms the Torah, and brings the gospel. Both revelations are approved for guidance and light (5:46).

John the Baptist quotes the prophet Isaiah (40:3) to announce the appearance of Jesus:

> Behold, I send my messenger before your face, who shall prepare your way;
> the voice of one crying in the wilderness: Prepare the way of the Lord, make
> his paths straight. (Mark 1:2,3)

Peter, once a wavering follower of Jesus, is the transformed preacher on the day of Pentecost when he calls upon the faithful Jews in the temple to follow the Way of the Messiah. "Save yourselves from this crooked generation" (Acts 2:40). Three thousand souls respond and are baptized, which is accompanied by the apostles' guidance, "fellowship" and the "breaking of bread and prayers" (2:41,42).

The Letter to the Hebrews asks the believers to strengthen their walk in Christ by lifting up "drooping hands and weak knees" to prepare "straight paths for your feet" (12:12,13). A second metaphor is employed to heighten a spiritual life of peace and holiness to obtain God's grace, that "no root of bitterness spring up and cause trouble" (Heb. 12:15). A third set of images appears in the writer's discussion of the calamity that overcame Esau in his selling of his birthright to his brother Jacob (Gen. 27:1f). All of these metaphors in Hebrews stress the selection of good over evil guidance.

The apostolic leadership of Paul provides ample guides for the young churches he founded. His letter to the Philippian church praises them for "shining as lights in the world" and avoiding the "crooked and perverse generation" that surrounded them (Phil. 2:14). To the Ephesians, he says, "But you are light in the Lord; walk as children of light" (Eph. 5:8).

Meditation: I find myself between a desire to please myself and a desire to follow Your path, O Holy God. Continually grant me good guidance.

Exodus 15:13   Isaiah 58:11   John 16:33   Acts 8:31   1 Thessalonians 3:11

99 Beautiful Names of God

99 The Patient One   ٱلصَّبُورُ AṢ-ṢABŪR

For I knew that you are a gracious God and merciful, slow to anger, and abounding in steadfast love, and repenting of evil. Jonah 4:2

"It is grace that brought me safe thus far and grace will lead me home" completes the last stanza of "Amazing Grace."[1] Nowhere is that grace more evident than in God's patient dealings with the creation, and nowhere is God's mercy more apparent among his creatures than when they respond with patience toward one another. The servant of God, one who rightly deserves to be called the servant of the Patient God, is admonished by the apostle James, who connects the prophets with endurance and God's compassion:

> As an example of suffering and patience, [my fellow servants], take the prophets who spoke in the name of the Lord. Lo, we call those blessed who were patient. You have heard of the patience of Job, and you have seen the purpose of the Lord, how the Lord is compassionate and merciful. (James 5:10,11)

Abraham, God's intimate friend, is hailed in Hebrews as one who "having patiently endured, obtained the promise" (6:15). This same epistle lists over a score of men and women from the Hebrew text who lived a life of faith and hope for God's final salvation. The list in chapter 11 begins with Abel and ends with a number of nameless heroes and heroines "of whom the world was not worthy" (38); and even though they exercised great faith, they "did not receive what was promised" (39). This great cloud of witnesses that includes Noah, Jacob, Moses, Samuel, David and the harlot Rahab, is cited to encourage the Hebrew readers to "lay aside every weight, and sin" and "run with patience the race that is set before" them (12:1).

The greatest model of patient endurance is Jesus, "the pioneer and perfecter of our faith," who is further honored as the one who "endured the cross, despising the shame, and is seated on the right hand of the throne of God" (12:2).

The Arabic word for patience is a favorite in the Arabic Bible and has several verbal offshoots in the Qur'an. The citation here is from Dawood's translation:[2]

> We gave Moses our guidance and the Israelites the Book to inherit; a guide and an admonition to me of understanding. Therefore have patience; God's promise is true. Implore forgiveness for your sins, and celebrate the praise of your Lord evening and morning. (Sura 40:52)

The Hebrew Bible does not contain this word but there are numerous examples, along with the New Covenant citations above, of God's showing patience toward his created world. God's eternal endurance helps the Merciful One to overcome the capriciousness of humankind when he "always is slow to anger" (Ps. 86:15).

This list of 99 names begins with mercy and ends with patience. The apostle Paul has a short list with these two names in the opening and closing position. "As God's chosen ones" put on mercy and patience (Col. 3:12).

Meditation: My humble thanks go up to You, O Patient and Loving Heavenly Father. And yes, give me patience. Amen.

Psalm 103:8 Ecclesiastes 7:8 Romans 12:12 2 Timothy 2:24 James 1:3 Revelation 1:9

---

[1] John Newton, no. 209.
[2] The Koran, p. 332.

SELECTED BIBLIOGRAPHY

A. Major Reference Works

Brown, Francis, S. R. Driver and Charles Briggs, eds. *Hebrew and English Lexicon of the Old Testament*. Oxford: Clarendon Press, 1959.

Kassis, Hanna. *A Concordance of the Qur'an*. Berkeley: University of California Press, 1983.

Wehr, Hans. *A Dictionary of Modern Written Arabic*. Wiesbaden, Germany: Harrassowitz, 1961.

Young, Robert. *Analytical Concordance to the Bible*. Grand Rapids: Eerdmans, n.d.

B. General

Al-Ghazali. *The Ninety-Nine Beautiful Names of God*. Trans. David B. Burrell and Nazih Daher. Cambridge: Islamic Texts Society, 1992.

Ali, Abdullah Yusuf. *The Holy Qur'an: Text, Translation and Commentary*. New York: Hafner Publishing Company, 1946.

Arndt, William F. and Wilbur Gingrich. *A Greek-English Lexicon of the New Testament and Other Early Christian Literature*. Chicago: University of Chicago Press, 1952.

Asad, Muhammad, trans. *The Message of the Qur'an*. Gibraltar: Dar al-Andalus, 1984.

Chittick, William C. *The Sufi Path of Love*. Albany, NY: SUNY Press, 1983.

Colledge, Edmund, and Bernard McGinn, trans. *Meister Eckhart: The Essential Sermons, Commentaries, Treatises and Defense*. New York: Paulist Press, 1981.

Cragg, Kenneth. "Christians Among Muslims." *Evangelical Review of Theology*, 20, 2. (April 1996).

Dahood, Mitchell. *Psalms*. Vols. 2, 3. Garden City, NY: Doubleday and Company, 1970.

Dawood, N. J., trans. The Koran. 5th ed. New York: Penguin Books, 1990.

Edmunds, Lidie. "My Faith Has Found a Resting Place." In *Hymns*. Comp. and ed., Paul Beckwith. Chicago: Inter-Varsity Press, 1952.

Glasse, Cyril. *The Concise Encyclopedia of Islam*. New York: Harper and Row, 1989.

Goldziher, Ignaz. *Introduction to Islamic Theology and Law*. Princeton: University Press, 1981.

Ibn Al 'Arabi. *The Bezels of Wisdom*. Trans. R. W. J. Austin. New York: Paulist Press, 1980.

Muggeridge, Malcolm. *Something Beautiful for God*. New York: Ballantine Books, 1973.

Newton, John. "Amazing Grace." In *The Methodist Hymnal*. New York: The Methodist Publishing House, 1939.

Schimmel, Annemarie. *Islamic Names*. Edinburgh: University Press, 1989.

Smith, George Adam. *Jeremiah: The Baird Lecture for 1922*. 4th ed. New York: Harper and Brothers, n.d.

Sweetman, J. Windrow. *Islam and Christian Theology*. Part 1, vols. 1 and 2: *Origins*. London: Lutterworth Press, 1947.

Zwemer, Samuel. *Studies in Popular Islam*. London: Sheldon Press, 1939.

SUBJECT INDEX

ABRAHAM, 34, 68, 94
    Abraham and Isaac, 20, 32, 33, 66, 90
    In the New Testament, 2, 13, 29, 40, 48, 62, 63, 66, 72, 99
    In the Old Testament, 3, 6, 12, 26, 29, 35, 40, 42, 55, 57, 69, 76, 84, 88, 92, 93
ADAM, 11, 12, 13, 14, 19, 31, 44, 60, 70
AL-GHAZALI, 15, 70, 77, 95
ARAMAIC, 7, 16, 49, 52, 75, 78, 86, 87
DAVID, 9, 34, 45, 60
    In the New Testament, 2, 40, 56, 99
    The King, 7, 15, 28, 31, 32, 42, 43, 46, 53, 61, 65, 69, 77, 84, 90, 95, 97
    The Psalmist, 6, 8, 12, 19, 27, 29, 30, 39, 40, 51, 64, 71, 75, 79, 92, 96
HEBREW (See also Book of Hebrews)
    Bible (Old Testament), 1, 3, 6, 7, 8, 9, 13, 22, 27, 30, 34, 37, 39, 41, 44, 48, 50, 54, 59, 61, 64, 68, 70, 80, 88, 89, 90, 96, 99
    Hebrew Words, 6, 7, 11, 13, 14, 15, 16, 18, 19, 20, 21, 22, 24, 25, 26, 28, 29, 31, 35, 36, 38, 39, 40, 41, 42, 45, 46, 47, 48, 49, 51, 52, 53, 56, 57, 60, 61, 63, 65, 67, 69, 71, 72, 73, 74, 75, 76, 79, 80, 81, 82, 84, 86, 87, 88, 93
HOLY SPIRIT, 4, 5, 8, 9, 30, 45, 50, 52, 53, 67, 74, 76, 79, 89, 94, 96, 97
IBN ARABI, 33, 73
ISRAEL
    Kingdom of Israel, 4, 13, 19, 21, 24, 30, 31, 34, 38, 41, 42, 53, 58, 59, 65, 75, 77, 78, 93, 97
    New Covenant, 49, 53, 67, 74, 87, 89, 96
    Tribes of Israel, 6, 8, 23, 28, 29, 34, 36, 43, 45, 48, 63, 72, 74, 77, 82
JERUSALEM, 2, 4, 5, 6, 7, 9, 11, 12, 15, 19, 26, 27, 28, 31, 34, 38, 43, 44, 46, 48, 50, 52, 54, 58, 70, 72, 78, 81, 83, 84, 86, 87, 88, 89, 92, 94, 96, 97
    Also, see TEMPLE
JESUS, 11, 12, 29
    Birth, 36, 48, 65, 66, 71, 84
    Death and Resurrection, 4, 15, 19, 33, 34, 48, 49, 55, 62, 63, 65, 66, 83, 89
    "I Am", 51, 62, 93, 94 (summary)
    In Coming Days, 3, 56, 68, 71, 85
    Jesus and Holy Spirit, 4, 45, 51, 52, 59, 74, 89, 94, 96
    Jesus in the Qur'an, 23, 45, 58, 63, 65, 74, 76, 95, 97, 98
    Miracles, 6, 34, 59, 60, 61, 78, 84, 90

JESUS (Continued)
    Servant of God – (Suffering Servant), 1, 5, 18, 23, 28, 33, 40, 44, 45, 48, 66, 70, 79, 83, 86, 91
    Teaching – Parables, 2, 6, 7, 16, 18, 19, 26, 30, 32, 37, 39, 44, 46, 50, 51, 52, 53, 54, 55, 57, 63, 64, 73, 74, 75, 76, 77, 79, 80, 81, 82, 84, 87, 88, 92, 93, 97, 98, 99
KORAN, see QUR'AN
LAZARUS, 60, 61, 63
MIRIAM, see MARY
NEBUCHADNEZZAR, 16, 22, 42, 78, 86
NEWTON, John, 1, 99
PHARISEES, 33, 74, 76, 79
PROPHETS
    Aaron, 8, 43, 54, 65, 69, 72
    Abraham, 32, 33, 34
    Adam, 11, 12, 13, 14
    David, 2, 6, 7, 8, 28, 29, 30, 31, 32, 33, 34, 39, 45, 51, 53, 56, 60, 61, 64, 65, 69, 71, 75, 77, 79, 90, 95, 96, 99
    Elijah, 42, 43, 44, 48, 59, 72, 73
    Isaac, 20, 32, 33, 42, 48, 62, 66, 72, 76, 90, 95
    Ishmael, 26, 33, 42, 66
    Jacob, 48, 50, 53, 62, 72, 75, 76, 90, 99
    John the Baptist, 21, 60, 79, 98
    Jonah, 6, 34, 85
    Joseph, 16, 17, 19, 40, 41, 46, 75, 90, 92
    Mary, 8, 23, 36, 58, 59, 61, 65, 74, 92, 98
    Moses, 1, 2, 4, 6, 8, 12, 14, 17, 19, 23, 25, 28, 33, 34, 35, 42, 45, 48, 55, 62, 63, 67, 72, 73, 74, 75, 76, 81, 92, 93, 94, 99
    Muhammad, 34
    Noah, 12, 34, 72, 78, 80, 90, 91, 99
QUR'AN
    Words and Quotations, 1, 2, 3, 4, 9, 11, 12, 20, 22, 27, 35, 47, 49, 55, 62, 63, 65, 68, 70, 72, 76, 78, 80, 93, 95
RUMI, 47, 62
SAMARITANS, 2, 16, 22, 25, 97
SAUL, 50, 80, 87
SOLOMON, 4, 14, 31, 33, 41, 46, 47, 48, 54, 65, 68, 77, 93
STEPHEN, 36, 48, 50, 92
TEMPLE, 4, 7, 12, 14, 15, 19, 27, 31, 35, 36, 44, 48, 54, 56, 57, 58, 68, 70, 79, 85, 87, 92, 93, 96, 98

SCRIPTURE INDEX

OLD TESTAMENT

Genesis
1:1 — 11
1:3 — 93
1:4 — 80
1:21,24 — 60
1:22 — 42
1:22, 25 — 11
1:26 — 44
1:27 — 13
1:28 —11, 15
2:7 — 60
2:19 — 44
2:20 — 11
3:7, 22 — 19
3:20 — 60
3:21 — 14
4:1 — 19
6:7 — 72
6:8 — 92
6:9 — 91
6:13,14 — 91
6:17 — 12
8:21 — 26
9:20 — 92
10:8, 9 — 9
13:2 — 88
13:6 — 89
14:17 — 84
14:19, 20 — 35
15:5, 7 — 93
15:6 — 6, 40, 57
15:17 — 93
16:2 — 90
16:8 — 9
16:11 — 26
17:2 — 42
17:20 — 42
18:3 — 92
18:18 — 33
18:19 — 29
21:33 — 68
22:2,12,16 — 66
22:9 — 20
22:13 — 33
22:17 — 42
27:1 — 98
30:2,24 — 90
30:31 — 39
31:50 — 50
32:25 — 26
34:30 — 87
37–50 — 16
37:18 — 10
39:5 — 41
40:1 — 75
41:35f — 46
41:51, 52 — 17
42:8 — 19
43:14 — 16
47:15 — 16
49:2 — 87
50:20 — 40

Exodus
3:2f — 93
3:3f — 62
3:13f — 76
3:21 — 92
6:2,3 — 76
10:2 — 19
12:24 — 51
13:2 — 18
13:22 — 93
14:13 — 75
14:21 — 8
14:30 — 45
14:31 — 6
15:2 — 8
16 — 17
18:11 — 33
19:6 — 77
20:3 — 67
20:5 — 43
20:6 — 30
20:16 — 50
20:17 — 56
20:24 — 35
24:16 — 48
28:3 — 46
30:10 — 14
32:14 — 72
32:30, 31 — 14
33:11 — 55
35:25 — 46

Leviticus
3–4 — 5
4:1-7 — 19
5:10 — 82
7:1-10 —12
19:18 — 81
21:11 — 61
24:1f — 93
26:23f — 81

Numbers
13:28 — 8
14:8 — 38
21:9 — 23
25:11 — 43

Deuteronomy
4:32f — 12
4:38 — 33
5:7 — 11
5:16 — 24
5:26 — 62
6:4 — 67
7:9 — 6
7:13 — 42
8:3 — 17
10:17 — 29
11:5,6 — 91
11:12 — 27
11:24 — 72
18:15 — 3, 45
19:15 — 50
24:21 — 87
26:15 — 36
30:19 — 69
31:20 — 17
32:4 — 29, 51
32:29 — 74
32:36 — 28
32:43 — 81
33:4, 5 — 77
33:5 — 28
33:13f — 65
33:13, 14, 16 — 48
33:26 — 10

Joshua
3:10 — 60
4:9 — 63
10:2 — 9
13:33 — 97
16:10 — 97
24:20 — 91
24:27 — 50

Judges
4:4 — 28
8:23 — 77
10:8 — 97
16:5f — 53

Ruth
1:15f — 97
2:13 — 92
4:4f — 63
4:9f — 50

1 Samuel
2:3 — 21
2:6 — 61
2:6, 7 — 23
2:30 — 24
4:21 — 48
7:6 — 28
8:20 — 28
10:24 — 69
12:5 — 50
15:29 — 80
17:51 — 9
20:15 — 30
22:1 — 29
30:4 — 53

2 Samuel
5:2 — 39
7:26 — 65
8:15 — 28
11:3 — 97
12:9, 12 — 31
14:20 — 46
16:17 — 30
18:20 — 31
19:2 — 15
20:16 — 46
22:6 — 61
22:47 — 60
23:10, 12 — 15

1 Kings
7:41 — 85
7:48 — 93
8:36 — 14
12:33 — 58
17:8f — 59
18 — 43
18:19f — 42

99 Beautiful Names of God

SCRIPTURE INDEX (Continued)

18:37 — 44
19:12 — 44
19:14 — 43
19:18 — 43
20:31 — 30

2 Kings
5:1 — 59
5:1, 3 — 9
19:22 — 67
19:31 — 72

1 Chronicles
11:4, 5 — 97
15:16, 17 — 7
16:41 — 79
17:3 — 31
21:8 — 31
21:18f — 97
25:1 — 7
27:32 — 47
29:25 — 65

2 Chronicles
2:12 — 31
3:3 — 68
6:23 — 28
7:1 — 48
7:14 — 14
13:12 — 73
20:7 — 55
21:8-10 — 97
23:5 — 54
28:24 — 87
28:25 — 97
31:21 — 51

Ezra
3:6 — 68
3:11 — 54
5:5 — 27
9:15 — 87
10:1 — 35

Nehemiah
1:5 — 38
5:18 — 79
6:8 — 58
9:6,10,16,17 — 34
9:25,26 — 34
9:7 — 69
9:20 — 90

9:32 — 37
10:29 — 34
10:33 — 14

Esther
3:8 — 38
5:2 — 92
6:6 — 38
9:24 — 40
9:30 — 51

Job
1:7 — 44
1:12 — 44
1:19 — 10
3:10 — 76
9:2 — 44
9:6 — 21
14:14 — 49
18:20 — 72
19:25 — 44, 74
22:12 — 36
26:8 — 20
27—28 — 46
33:3 — 79
36:31 — 10
36:16 — 21
37:23 — 29, 37
38:15 — 90
38:18 — 21
42:5 — 26

Psalms
1:2, 4, 5, 6 — 98
1:6 — 19
2:4, 5 — 22
7:11 — 29
8:1 — 85
8:2 — 56
8:3, 4 — 68
8:4 — 23, 24
10:11 — 27
16:10, 11 — 61
18:50 — 75
19:9 — 79, 96
20:9 — 15
21:2 — 90
21:4 — 71
22:29 — 22
22:31 — 45
23:2 — 59
23:5 — 39

24:2 — 68
24:4 — 79
24:8 — 9
25:9 — 98
25:11 — 82
27:11 — 19
28:9 — 39
29:2 — 16
31:5 — 51
31:9 — 76
31:21 — 30
32:1, 2 — 40
33:5 — 30
34:8,10,12,14 — 80
34:14 — 5
34:15 — 27
35:4 — 95
35:20 — 95
35:27 — 65
37:3 — 97
37:11 — 97
40:11 — 6
40:17 — 40
42:7 — 41, 85
47:9 — 36
48:1, 2 — 4
50:2 — 41
50:10 — 88
60:8 — 97
62:11 — 81
62:11,12 — 2, 17, 30
65:7 — 53
65:9 — 88
65:11,12 — 83
66:5,7 — 77
68:18 — 56
70:4 — 65
71:2 — 36
71:2, 3 — 26
75:7 — 23
80:1 — 75
81:5,6 — 51
84:11 — 90
84:1, 2 — 47
86:5 — 82
86:16 — 8
88:1 — 7
88:6 — 22
88:11, 12 — 7
89:18 — 67
89:20 — 64
89:36 — 96
94:1,3 — 81

94:2 — 22
94:3,4 — 81
94:4,10 — 81
94:10 — 22
94:23 — 22
96:2 — 31
96:6 — 41
98:1 — 15
99:2, 3 — 37
101:3, 6 — 27
102:27, 28 — 96
103:2 — 92
103:8 — 1, 83
103:11 — 30
103:13 — 1
104:5 — 68
104:24,25 — 88
105:26 — 69
106:19 — 25
106:20 — 48
106:40 — 91
110:4 — 3
110:5 — 3
111:3 — 96
111:10 — 96
113:6, 7, 8, 9 — 32
116:5 — 2
116:14 — 5
116:16 — 18
116:17 — 35
119:5 — 51
119:8, 44, 57 — 38
119:17 — 42
119:75 — 28
119:134, 168 — 38
119:176 — 28, 39
121:4 — 38, 62
122:6 — 5
123:2 — 9
127:2 — 17, 47
132:11 — 51
138:3 — 8
138:4 — 84
139:1,2 — 19
139:1,23 — 64
139:7,8 — 64
139:13,16 — 64
145:16 — 18
146:8,9 — 59
147:1 — 56
147:9 — 39
147:19 — 75
148:1-5 — 56

SCRIPTURE INDEX (Continued)

Proverbs
3:19 — 68
6:17 — 10
6:25 — 56
6:34 — 43
8:18 — 88
8:22 — 71
11:1 — 86
15:20 — 46
16:11 — 86
17:17 — 55
18:8 — 76
22:2,4 — 88
22:22 — 86
30:8,9 — 88

Ecclesiastes
3:5 — 87
3:11 — 41, 96
12:14 — 41

Song of Solomon
2:8, 10 — 47
4:13 — 48
7:10 — 41

Isaiah
1:29 — 56
2:2,3 — 72
5:22 — 9
6:1 — 36, 48
6:9 — 26
7:14 — 66
8:7 — 33
8:19 — 61
9:6 — 5, 9
9:6,7 — 84
9:7 — 77
10:21 — 9
11:2 — 45
13:11 — 10
13:17 — 40
17:13 — 10
26:1 — 8
29:13 — 79
34:4 — 41, 85
38:12 — 20
38:19 — 60
39:8 — 51
40:3 — 98
40:11 — 39
41:14 — 67
41:15 — 58

41:23 — 74
42:1 — 70
42:5 — 21
43:1, 2 — 11
43:1, 7 — 13
43:20 — 24
43:21 — 13
44:6 — 73
44:28 — 39
45:1 — 18
45:8 — 83
45:9 — 12
45:21 — 29
47:3 — 81
47:4 — 67
48:13 — 68
49:2 — 79
49:5 — 24
50:5 — 18
52:10 — 18
52:11 — 79
52:13 — 23, 66
53:3 — 40
53:4f — 45
53:5 — 5
53:7 — 18
53:7,12 — 91
53:8,9 — 60
53:12 — 23, 40, 66
56:8 — 87
57:15 — 36
59:1 — 26
59:15 — 27
60:3 — 89
60:11 — 18
60:14 — 22
60:19 — 93
61:1,2 — 59
62:2 — 58, 89
65:16 — 51
65:17 — 11
66:3 — 69
66:19 — 89
66:22 — 58

Jeremiah
1:5 — 13, 70
1:16 — 97
3:7 — 80
4:30 — 88
5:9 — 81
9:9 — 81
9:10 — 85

9:23 — 88
9:24 — 38
10:10 — 62
10:12 — 53
12:10 — 85
13:16 — 93
15:4 — 41
15:6 — 91
15:15 — 32
15:19 — 25
15:21 — 91
17:12 — 36
23:3 — 87
26:3f — 72
31:33 — 4
31:34 — 19
32:18 — 8, 75
33:3 — 27, 76
33:6 — 51
33:22 — 42
50:19 — 39
51:11 — 79
52:32 — 30

Lamentations
1:12 — 83
2:2 — 83
3:23 — 6
3:49 — 83
4:13 — 12
5:2 — 97

Ezekiel
3:14 — 23
11:1 — 72
14:14, 20 — 78
20:5 — 69
23:6 — 56
28:8f — 61
31:15 — 90
32:12 — 10
34:11 — 39
34:23 — 39
37:24f — 77
39:7 — 4

Daniel
2:2, 27 — 87
2:6 — 75
2:21 — 16
2:37, 38 — 16
2:47 — 86
3:24 — 94

3:26 — 78
3:28f — 78
4:1 — 42
5:17 — 16
5:20 — 22
5:21 — 78
5:25 — 86
7:13 — 71
7:18 — 78
7:22 — 71, 78
7:25 — 78
8:1 — 85
8:17 — 49
9:6 — 80
9:9, 10 — 34
9:18, 19 — 26
12:2 — 49, 61
12:3 — 75
12:4 — 21

Hosea
3:4 — 12
4:6 — 21
7:10 — 80
11:1 — 66
13:14 — 62

Amos
2:4,6 — 82
4:1 — 88
4:6 — 17, 80
4:7 — 90
5:11 — 56, 85
5:15 — 29
5:20 — 93
8:5, 6 — 86
9:9, 10 — 82

Jonah
1:6 — 33
1:17 — 37
2:2, 6 — 61
3:5 — 6
3:9 — 80
4:2 — 37, 99

Micah
2:12 — 87
6:6 — 71
6:6, 8 — 36
7:5 — 55
7:18, 19 — 15

SCRIPTURE INDEX (Continued)

Habakkuk
1:5 — 6
2:2 — 27

Zephaniah
3:9 — 79

Haggai
2:18 — 68

Zechariah
1:3 — 80
1:14 — 43
4:6 — 69
7:11 — 26
8:8 — 51
9:6 — 10
12:10 — 71
14:9 — 3, 67

Malachi
1:6, 7 — 24
2:10 — 12, 67
3:1 — 38

NEW TESTAMENT

Matthew
1:21 — 45
1:23 — 66
3:1-13 — 79
3:2 — 80
4:4 — 17
4:17 — 3
5:5 — 97
5:20 — 74
5:39 — 81
6:10 — 77
6:10, 33 — 3
6:11, 12 — 17
6:33 — 89
7:1 — 28
7:14 — 74
8:11 — 72
8:17 — 5
9:2f — 34
9:6,8 — 53
9:30 — 18
9:38 — 42
10:1 — 53
10:5 — 96
10:20 — 96
10:22 — 96
11:20f — 9
11:29 — 22, 30
12:11 — 39
12:33 — 42
12:40,41 — 37
12:41, 42 — 33
13:5 — 54
13:14, 15 — 26
13:22 — 89
13:23, 31, 33 — 21
13:24f — 42
13:35 — 68, 69
13:44 — 89
17:11 — 59
17:14-20 — 52
18:22 — 82
21:9,15 — 56
21:16 — 56
22:13,14 — 74
22:23f — 63
22:32 — 62
23:23 — 82
23:27 — 74
23:34 — 46
23:37 — 83
24:13, 14 — 96
24:15 — 78
24:27 — 71
24:30 — 71
24:31 — 69
24:45 — 46
25:1f — 46, 93
25:21 — 6
25:31 — 88
25:34 — 3,68,69,97
25:40, 41 — 2
25:41 — 68
26:14 — 55
26:39 — 83, 84
26:65 — 34
27:46 — 83, 84
28:11,12 — 63
28:18 — 53
28:19f — 19

Mark
1:1 — 73
1:2, 3 — 21, 98
1:21 — 19
3:35 — 65
4:1 — 19
4:26 — 76
5:6, 7 — 36
5:7 — 78
7:6 — 79
7:22 — 10
9:8 — 73
9:35 — 73
9:42 — 73
10:15 — 73
10:21 — 80
10:24 — 73
10:30,31 — 73
10:42-45 — 77
10:45 — 1
11:9,10 — 56
12:29,32 — 67
13:3f — 96
14:24,25 — 58
14:44 — 55
14:51,52 — 73

Luke
1:13,59 — 60
1:15 — 37
1:32 — 36
1:43f — 65
1:47 — 65
1:51 — 8
1:76 — 36
2:7 — 71
2:9 — 48, 65
2:14 — 65
2:41 — 92
2:52 — 92
3:11 — 86
3:12,14 — 86
4:16f — 87
4:18, 21 — 88
4:19 — 21
4:41 — 90
6:6 — 87
6:10 — 59
6:20 — 97
6:22, 23 — 22
6:46 — 54
6:49 — 54
7:28 — 37
9:30, 31 — 48
9:58 — 84
10:29f — 2
10:37 — 2
11:4 — 61
11:39 — 79
13:4, 5 — 43
13:29 — 72
14:14 — 49
14:29,32 — 57
15:2 — 64
15:6, 9 — 64
15:18 — 18
15:30,32 — 64
16:19f — 63
16:31 — 63
17:21 — 76
18:9-14 — 57
18:18 — 52
18:22 — 52
18:25 — 52
18:27 — 52
19:28f — 9
19:39, 40 — 56
22:37 — 40, 91
22:42 — 66
22:44 — 83
22:69 — 84
22:70 — 67
23:40 — 86
23:43 — 86
24:26 — 48
24:44f — 66

John
1:1 — 11, 67
1:1, 2 — 58
1:1, 14 — 45
1:14 — 51, 66
1:17 — 1
1:30 — 37
2:23, 24 — 6
3:3 — 7
3:14 — 23
3:16 — 6, 47, 66
3:30 — 37
4:4 — 97
4:7, 10 — 16
4:24 — 51
4:37 — 68
4:44 — 25
5:26 — 62
5:29 — 49
6:32 — 16
6:48 — 17, 94
7:14 — 19
8:12 — 93, 94
8:32 — 51
8:39 — 66
8:49 — 25
8:51 — 38

SCRIPTURE INDEX (Continued)

9:24 — 90	3:13 — 48	11:22 — 25, 30	**Ephesians**
9:39 — 49	4:33 — 50	11:33 — 46	1:4 — 68
10:7 — 94	5:31 — 34	12:17 — 81	1:7, 8 — 89
10:11 — 94	5:32 — 52	12:19 — 81	1:12 — 95
10:14, 15, 16 — 39	6:1, 7 — 42	13:1 — 53	1:13, 14 — 4, 97
10:30 — 67	7:10 — 92	13:1-5 — 81	1:14 — 89
11:8 — 60	7:46 — 92	13:4 — 81	1:15 — 47
11:17 — 60	7:47 — 36	15:18, 19 — 9	1:17 — 46
11:25 — 63	7:55 — 48	16:19 — 46	1:22 — 87
11:26 — 60	7:58f — 50	16:27 — 46	2:7 — 89
11:42 — 60	8:28f — 5		2:10 — 12
11:45f — 60	8:33 — 91	**1 Corinthians**	2:19 — 89
12:13 — 56	8:35 — 18	1:20 — 46	3:6, 7 — 89
12:26 — 24	9:1 — 50	1:24 — 53	3:8-10 — 89
12:32, 33 — 23	9:2 — 50, 51, 87	2:9 — 27	3:9 — 12
13:11 — 79	9:20 — 87	3:10, 11, 12 — 54	3:11 — 95
13:16 — 33	13:20,22,23,26 — 2	3:13 — 54	3:16 — 8
14:1, 10 — 6	13:23 — 49	3:17 — 4	4:2 — 32
14:6 — 51, 62, 94	13:34,38 — 2	4:5 — 35	4:23, 24 — 12
14:10 — 75	13:48 — 70	11:23 — 6	5:8 — 98
14:15 — 38	16:16 — 78	13:1f — 47	5:25, 26 — 79
14:16, 17 — 51	16:17 — 36	13:1-3 — 41	6:2 — 24
14:25 — 4	17:22 — 76	13:13 — 41	
15:12, 13 — 55	17:30 — 34, 80	15:3,4 — 62	**Philippians**
15:15 — 55	19:9 — 94	15:20 — 63	1:11 — 42
15:26 — 4	22:4 — 50	15:22 — 13	2:5-8 — 13
15:26 — 75	22:16 — 79	15:45 — 13	2:7f — 5
16:8 — 74	22:20, 21 — 50	15:54 — 15, 62	2:9 — 23
16:13 — 75, 94	24:14f — 94	16:1 — 92	2:14 — 98
16:33 — 15	28:30 — 50	16:22 — 55	3:7, 8 — 40
17:22, 23 — 67			3:9 — 64
17:24 — 68, 69	**Romans**	**2 Corinthians**	4:13 — 52
18:20 — 44	1:3 — 6	1:15, 16 — 92	
18:38 — 51	1:4 — 66	4:7 — 53	**Colossians**
19:18 — 84	1:9 — 50	5:17 — 11	1:15 — 13
19:26, 27 — 65	1:24, 25 — 11	5:17, 18 — 49	1:15, 18 — 71
20:30, 31 — 66	2:4 — 32, 80	6:4, 8 — 25	1:18 — 71
20:31 — 62	2:11 — 29	6:6 — 30	1:20 — 57
21:15 — 39	2:29 — 35	6:6, 7 — 53	1:27 — 89
	3:25 — 32	6:11 — 18	3:12 — 99
Acts	4:3 — 40	9:10 — 42	3:12, 13 — 32
1:5, 6 — 79	4:7, 8 — 40	10:1 — 30	4:6 — 44
1:7, 8 — 53	4:13 — 6, 29	13:11 — 47	
1:8 — 50	5:2, 3 — 14		**1 Thessalonians**
2:1-21 — 79	6:23 — 68	**Galatians**	2:5f — 90
2:14,16,25,34 — 27	7:12 — 4	2:6 — 29	
2:17f — 74	8:15,16 — 76	3:6f — 29	**2 Thessalonians**
2:23, 24 — 70	8:23 — 71	5:22 — 5, 42	2:6, 7 — 90
2:38 — 80	8:28 — 95	6:1 — 59	
2:40 — 98	8:29 — 69, 95	6:14 — 47	**1 Timothy**
2:41, 42 — 98	9:11 — 95	6:15, 16 — 49	1:2 — 5
2:47 — 92	11:2 — 69	6:22 — 30	6:1 — 92
3:6 — 54	11:5 — 72		

SCRIPTURE INDEX (Continued)

6:13 — 84
6:15 — 3, 84
6:19 — 68

2 Timothy
1:2 — 5
1:10 — 75
2:8, 9 — 20
2:29 — 54
3:10, 11 — 95

Titus
1:2, 3 — 75
3:8 — 92

Philemon
18 — 57

Hebrews
1:2 — 97
1:13 — 33
2:7, 8 — 24
2:10 — 58
2:15 — 61
3:3 — 33
3:6 — 54
3:7 — 25
4:3 — 68
5:5, 6 — 84
5:6 — 3
6:15 — 99

8:10 — 19
9:11, 12 — 14
9:11-14 — 33
9:14 — 68
10:12 — 33
11:8 — 97
11:38, 39 — 99
12:1, 2 — 99
12:12, 13 — 98
12:14 — 4, 5
12:15 — 98
12:24 — 58
13:1 — 47
13:15 — 56

James
1:18 — 71
1:22 — 26
2:23 — 55
2:24 — 29
4:10 — 23
5:10, 11 — 99
5:17 — 59

1 Peter
1:2 — 42
1:4 — 97
1:20 — 68
1:21 — 48
1:24 — 48
2:18 — 30

2:23 — 28
3:8 — 47
4:10 — 52
5:1 — 48
5:5, 6 — 10

2 Peter
1:2 — 42
1:17 — 47
3:8, 9 — 72
3:9f — 61

1 John
1:2 — 62
2:16 — 27
3:8 — 48
3:16 — 62
4:4 — 15
4:8 — 47
5:2 — 38

2 John
9 — 19

3 John
11 — 80

Jude
2 — 42
25 — 48

Revelation
1:1 — 85
1:5 — 50
1:7 — 71
1:8 — 73
1:9 — 45
2:5 — 80
2:8 — 74
3:14 — 7
3:19 — 80
3:20 — 18
4:2 — 85
5:8 — 85
5:12 — 53
6:1f — 85
6:16 — 85
7:10 — 85
7:17 — 39, 85
11:17 — 35
15:4 — 75
17:14 — 84
19:5 — 56
20:12 — 28
20:15 — 64

INDEX OF NAMES — ENGLISH AND ARABIC

ENGLISH	ARABIC	NUMBER
Abaser	*Al-Khāfiḍ*	22
Accepter of Repentance, Ever-relenting	*At-Tawwāb*	80
All Knowing	*Al-'Alīm*	19
All Powerful, Decreer	*Al-Qādir*	69
All Powerful, Determiner	*Al-Muqtadir*	70
All Seeing	*Al-Baṣīr*	27
Avenger	*Al-Muntaqim*	81
Aware One	*Al-Khabīr*	31
Beloved, Affection	*Al-Wadūd*	47
Beneficent, Sustainer, Gracious	*Ar-Raḥmān*	1
Bestower, Giver of Gifts	*Al-Wahhāb*	16
Bountiful One	*Al-Karīm*	42
Clement, Forbearing	*Al-Ḥalīm*	32
Compassionate	*Ar-Ra'ūf*	83
Creator	*Al-Khāliq*	11
Delayer, Postponer	*Al-Mu'akhkhir*	72
Dishonorer	*Al-Muzill*	25
Distresser, Destroyer	*Aḍ-Ḍārr*	91
Embracing One, Saving One	*Al-Wāsi'*	45
Enabler, Trustee	*Al-Wakīl*	52
Enduring, Everlasting	*Al-Bāqī*	96
Enricher	*Al-Mughnī*	89
Equitable	*Al-Muqsiṭ*	86
Eternal	*Aṣ-Ṣamad*	68
Ever-living, Alive	*Al-Ḥayy*	62
Exalter	*Ar-Rāfi'*	23
Expander, Widener	*Al-Bāsiṭ*	21
Faithful One	*Al-Mu'min*	6
Fashioner	*Al-Muṣawwir*	13
Finder	*Al-Wājid*	64
Firm One	*Al-Matīn*	54
First	*Al-Awwal*	73
Forgiver	*Al-Ghaffār*	14
Gatherer	*Al-Jāmeʿ*	87
Giver of Death	*Al-Mumīt*	61
Giver of Life	*Al-Muḥyi*	60
Glorious, Magnificent One	*Al-Mājid*	65
Governor, Ruler	*Al-Walī*	77
Great, Eminent One	*Al-Kabīr*	37
Great Forgiver	*Al-Ghafūr*	34
Guide	*Al-Hādi*	94
Hearer	*As-Samī'*	26
Highest One	*Al-Muta'alī*	78
Holy	*Al-Quddūs*	4
Honorer	*Al-Mu'izz*	24
Incomparable, Purpose Setter	*Al-Badī'*	95
Inheritor	*Al-Wārith*	97
Inner, Hidden	*Al-Bāṭin*	76
Jealous Guardian	*Ar-Raqīb*	43

111

99 Beautiful Names of God

Judge	Al-Ḥakam	28
Just	Al-'Adl	29
Kind One, Gentle One	Al-Laṭīf	30
King Over All Earthly Kingdoms	Mālik-ul-Mulk	84
King, Sovereign	Al-Malik	3
Last	Al-Ākhir	74
Light	An-Nūr	93
Maker, Creator	Al-Bāri'	12
Manifest	Aẓ-Ẓāhir	75
Merciful	Ar-Raḥīm	2
Mighty One	Al-'Aẓīm	33
Mighty One, Compeller	Al-Jabbār	9
Most Glorious	Al-Majīd	48
Most Great, Proud	Al-Mutakabbir	10
Most High	Al-'Alī	36
Nourisher	Al-Muqīt	39
One	Al-Aḥad	67
One Who Advances, Expediter	Al-Muqaddim	71
Opener	Al-Fattāḥ	18
Originator, Innovator	Al-Mubdī	58
Overcomer, Subduer	Al-Qahhār	15
Pardoner	Al-'Afuw	82
Patient One	Aṣ-Ṣabūr	99
Peaceful One	As-Salām	5
Possessor of Sublimity and Generosity	Dhūl-Jalāl-wal-Ikrām	85
Powerful	Al-Qawī	53
Praiseworthy	Al-Ḥamīd	56
Preserver	Al-Ḥafīẓ	38
Preventer, Delayer	Al-Māni'	90
Propitious, One Who Grants Favor	An-Nāfi'	92
Protecting Friend	Al-Walī	55
Protector	Al-Muhaymin	7
Provider	Ar-Razzāq	17
Reckoner	Al-Ḥasīb	40
Reconciler	Al-Muḥṣī	57
Responsive One	Al-Mujīb	44
Resurrector	Al-Bā'ith	49
Restorer	Al-Mu'īd	59
Restrainer, Binder	Al-Qābiḍ	20
Right Guide	Ar-Rashīd	98
Righteous, Pure	Al-Barr	79
Self Sufficient, Rich One	Al-Ghanī	88
Self-subsisting, Resurrected One	Al-Qayyūm	63
Strong One	Al-'Azīz	8
Sublime	Al-Jalīl	41
Thankful One	Ash-Shakūr	35
Truth	Al-Ḥaqq	51
Unique One	Al-Wāḥid	66
Wise	Al-Ḥakīm	46
Witness	Ash-Shahīd	50

www.ingramcontent.com/pod-product-compliance
Lightning Source LLC
Chambersburg PA
CBHW070459090426
42735CB00012B/2618